MW00782863

Murder Gone Cold

The Mystery of the Grimes Sisters

By

Tamara Shaffer

Till life forget and death remember,
Till thou remember and I forget

The small slain body, the flower-like face,
Can I remember if thou forget?

Thou hast forgotten, O summer swallow,
But the world shall end when I forget.

From a poem by Algernon
Charles Swinburne

This book is dedicated to a large number of loving, supportive persons who have encouraged my creativity and made my life better by their presence.

- Linda Strothman, treasured friend who has patiently driven to and trudged through graveyards and death sites and never even rolled her eyes
- John Stokes, her husband, who rolls his eyes only when I'm not looking
- Sandy Pittman, thoughtful, precious friend and gentle editor
- Bill Helmer, loving partner in crime
- Richard Lindberg, friend and the writer I want to be, who urged me to write this book and offered any help I needed
- Sheila Cronin, for her friendship and support
- Larry Raeder, for his tireless driving to points of interest and who deserves half the proceeds from this book for gas money
- Jerilyn Miripol, friend and poetic influence
- Colleen Fahy, friend and fellow writer and advisor
- Linda Modrowski, friend who shared her recollections
- Jim Graczyk, who cheered me on from cyberspace
- All interviewees who made the book possible by contributing their painful and poignant memories

And…a special thanks to Mark Sanders.

Copyright © 2006 Tamara Shaffer
All Rights Reserved, including the right to copy or
reproduce the book, or portions thereof, in any form, without
express written permission of the author and publisher.

Original Cover Artwork Designed by
Jim Graczyk
Ghost Guides
http://www.ghostguides.com

This Book is published by
Ghost Research Society Press
P. O. Box 205
Oak Lawn, Illinois 60454
(708) 425-5163
http://www.ghostresearch.org

ISBN: 0-9766072-7-1

Printed in the United States of America

INDEX

INTRODUCTION

Every time I see a murder in the news I think of the Grimes sisters, Barbara and Patricia, two girls who went to a movie one night and never came home. I didn't know Barbara and Patricia, but at the time of their shocking deaths, I lived within ten blocks of them and shared a parish and probably an array of trolleys and buses, stores, and entertainment venues.

It was 1956. In the throes of adolescence, I was less than happy about being relocated from a small town in northeastern Kentucky to this sprawling mass of concrete—purported home of gangsters and other criminals. It didn't improve my perspective to hear, immediately upon my arrival, about some grisly murders in Chicago's recent history.

William Heirens, a young University of Chicago student, was almost ten years into a life sentence for the murders, in 1945, of two North Side women and of six-year-old Suzanne Degnan just after the 1946 New Year. One woman was stabbed and the other stabbed and shot. The little girl had been stolen from her own bedroom on the morning of January 7th, and over the next few days, parts of her dismembered body were fished out of various neighborhood sewers piece by piece.

In October 1955, thirteen-year-old John Schuessler, his eleven-year-old brother, Anton, Jr., and their friend, Robert Peterson, also thirteen, had attended a movie in the Loop, then disappeared, their battered bodies found two days later in a forest preserve. That case had yet to be solved.

It felt ominous, then, when Barbara and Patricia Grimes disappeared right after Christmas. When the newspapers screamed out the discovery of their frozen bodies nearly a month later, an atmosphere of horror hovered over the city like a thick fog. Parents kept children inside, issuing stranger-danger warnings with new intensity. It was several weeks before the case failed to headline the front pages of Chicago's four daily newspapers.

Eight months later, when the Grimes sensation had died down considerably and the city's collective guard diminished, the body parts of fifteen-year-old Judith Mae Andersen were found divided between two oil drums floating in Montrose Harbor. She'd been visiting a friend, her late night walk home interrupted by someone in a car, who picked her up and shot her through the temple.

The ensuing years shocked us anew with nurse killer Richard Speck, killer of boys John Wayne Gacy, and neighboring Milwaukee's

Jeffrey Dahmer, who chose victims from the streets of Chicago, as did Indiana's homosexual killer Larry Eyler. As stunned as we were by their grisly deeds, we could at least feel a sense of closure when they were convicted, and one by one, followed their victims into eternity. Speck, Dahmer, and Eyler made headlines anew when they died in prison; Gacy's execution by lethal injection in 1994 garnered minute-by-minute media attention.

Chance, timing, and crafty police work closed the books on several notorious Chicago murders. Helen Vorhees Brach, never quite out of the news after her disappearance in 1977, was declared legally dead, even without a body, at the hands of William Bailey, an associate of sociopathic stable owner and equine profiteer Silas Jayne. The Schuessler-Peterson case was solved and again made headlines, forty years after the fact, with the arrest and conviction, in 1995, of Kenneth Hansen, another member of Jayne's corrupt equestrian community.

As other cases resurface, along with William Heirens' annual plea for freedom and a second conviction for Hansen, we still don't know who killed Barbara and Patricia Grimes. Even basic questions such as where, how, and why they were killed were never answered with certainty. Mentioned only in passing during the coverage of Hansen's first trial, this mystery that marked my teen years has no new clues, no suspects to question, and no startling developments to announce on television. All we have are memories and the same tired theories, full of contradiction, that were afloat the year it occurred.

This was a case that altered lives. It built the career of an unknown attorney and destroyed the political aspirations of a sheriff. A coroner's assistant lost his job over conflicts with other authorities, the public lost faith in dueling officials, and a community mile from the city was left with strange hauntings and apparitions. Yet, with all its fervor and impact, we still don't know if this seemingly perfect crime was the result of a brilliant, well-planned scheme or a spontaneous happenstance carried off by benefit of miraculous timing. Now approaching its fiftieth year, it is considered by many to be the most puzzling case in Illinois history.

Following is what I know about the murders of Barbara and Patricia Grimes. My account is short; it is missing a definite perpetrator, a trial, and witnesses willing to have their words made public. Many who might have shared information have grown silent, either from memories that have dimmed with time or through death.

The Era

"Idealists tend to view the 1950s as America's last golden age.... In truth, the Eisenhower years were never as blissful as depicted in the popular media...."

> Richard Lindberg,
> Author
> *Return to the Scene of the Crime*

Mention the 1950s and you're likely to conjure up images of dads with lunch pails, moms in curlers kissing them good-bye at the door, and carefree kids playing tag and spinning hula-hoops until dark. Touted posthumously as a time of peace, prosperity, and great family values, the decade emerges in reality as a time of great paradox.

During the first three years of the 1950s the country was involved in a bloody conflict in Korea that claimed the lives of over 30,000 of our sons, fathers, and brothers and was never resolved. As the decade progressed, civil rights and gender equality battles brewed beneath the surface and promised to erupt into chaos. The time was approaching for us to pay for our sins of exclusion and discrimination, but in the minds of many, the greatest threat was a distant red menace, and working class

Americans forged ahead prayerfully, striving to educate their children and furnish their modest homes with the steady stream of newly invented products and appliances that promised easier, more recreative living.

Housewives, who "manned" their kitchens almost exclusively and whose aprons represented feminine fulfillment, could now prepare a meal's starchy item with Minute Rice in the time it took to boil water, or pop a Swanson's complete frozen dinner[1] into the oven. Permanent press clothing reduced time at the ironing board, and Metracal diet drink, introduced in 1959, eliminated the complicated calorie counting of weight-loss efforts.

Nearly everyone had a telephone—with a dial—and it was black, rendered stationary with a six-foot cord attached permanently to the wall. Numbers in most large cities had expanded to five digits, preceded by a two-letter exchange.

Television had caught on and was fast becoming a household staple. For those of higher means, color sets were introduced in 1954,[2] costing nearly $1,200.00, but typically, the house television was a black-

---

[1] The first Swanson TV dinner, which sold for about one dollar, was turkey with cornbread dressing and gravy, sweet potatoes, and buttered peas. The frozen meal concept originated in 1953 with Gerry Thomas, a gourmet cook who never ate his own invention.

[2] On March 25, 1954, RCA announced the production of color television sets.

and-white floor model, its screen minute by today's standards, its fare innocuous. Lucille Ball, portraying the wifely buffoon to patient hubby, Ricky Riccardo, broke bold new ground by sharing her pregnancy with the nation, and Jackie Gleason issued hollow "to the moon" threats to his equally long-suffering wife, Alice, in *The Honeymooners*. These satires, juxtaposed against Ozzie and Harriet, the fifties' preferred template for domestic life, entertained hard-working parents after dinner, and Mousketeers competed with homework for the after-school attention of their offspring.

Prepubescent boys, in training to serve as sole financial support of their future families, could be seen during predawn hours tossing newspapers onto porches. High school girls took shorthand and typing for jobs to tide them over until they caught husbands, and Americans paid at least lip service to chastity before marriage. Female waists were cinched and skirts billowed; the properly attired lady completed her ensemble with a hat and white gloves.

Nuns still wore complicated, flowing habits of black and white, and Catholics paid special homage to the Mother of God in her persona as Our Lady of Fatima, whose purportedly grim message to three small children, delivered on a hillside in Portugal in 1917, was to be revealed by the Pope at the decade's end. The anticipated revelation, assumed to portend doom and destruction by the Russians, created a subtle undercurrent of dread among the Faithful, while the population at large built bomb shelters amid threats of nuclear destruction. While these fears detracted from the utopian perceptions of American life, the emergence of a new music called rock 'n roll threatened its virtuous image.

Sociologists, who had issued warnings that television would destroy the initiative and morals of America's children, joined parents in collective alarm, as a former truck driver from Memphis, Tennessee, named Elvis Presley, appeared on the September 9, 1956, *Ed Sullivan Show*.[3] Presley's earthy replications of rhythm and blues songs from the Delta paved a bridge for black rock 'n rollers to enter the mainstream and changed American popular music forever. Presley, as well as the earthy genre in general, was considered by many an insidious evil. Sullivan, absent for the actual performance due to an injury in a car accident,[4] prudently employed a two-pronged stipulation that Presley minimize his hip-swinging antics, before a teenage audience urged to curtail its collective enthusiasm.

---

[3] This was actually not Presley's first appearance on national television; the first was on *The Dorsey Brothers Stage Show*, on which he appeared six times. He then appeared on *The Steve Allen Show*, on which he performed "Hound Dog" to a real live Basset.
[4] Elvis was introduced by Charles Laughton standing in for Ed Sullivan.

Americans appeared less vexed about the influence of shapely former orphan Norma Jean Baker, who, breathless and half-dressed and renamed Marilyn Monroe, made her way into movies. Monroe, whose marriages and emotional upheavals provided fodder for gossip columns and newsreels until her death in 1962, contrasted with cool, classy actress Grace Kelly, who more accurately fit the fifties' feminine prototype. Kelly, who relinquished her position as Hollywood leading lady in the name of true love, provided just as much whimsy in her newly acquired role as Princess of Monaco, and Americans awaited the birth of her first baby, due just after the 1957 New Year.

In the sprawling metropolis of Chicago, Illinois, that event would be marred and nearly overlooked by one that would give a small Southwest Side community top billing.

"We don't hit people with baseball bats in McKinley Park."

> Comment from life-long McKinley Parker, 2000.

Nowhere was the fifties dream of work and success more clearly embodied than in Chicago's Southwest Side community of McKinley Park. While often not distinguished from Bridgeport on the east and Brighton Park on the west, it lay between the two, and like most of the city's early settlements, it emerged from its prominent industries, some of which were relocated from other areas after the fire of 1871.

In the 1880s there were nearly thirty brick-making yards on the banks of the Chicago River, and around 1990, William Wrigley built a gum factory at 35th Street and Ashland Avenue in the midst of America's first planned industrial park. This joint venture of the Chicago Union Stock Yards Company and the Chicago Junction Railway was followed, during World War I, by a peak in stockyard meat production. With that, and the *Chicago Sun-Times* publishing and distribution plant west of

Ashland Avenue along the river, there was no dearth of jobs for the Bohemian, Polish, and Irish immigrants on the community's northern edge, nor for the Germans and Poles south of 31st Street.

A large number of the progeny of these early settlers remained proudly in McKinley Park in 1957, continuing to thrive on local industries. Despite the technological age, well under way, Chicago was still a factory town. Blue-collar paychecks, averaging $90 a week, might have provided Sunday tickets to Riverview Amusement Park at Belmont and Western Avenues, accessible by the Western Avenue trolley, or school clothes from Sears at Englewood Shopping Center at 63rd and Halsted Streets. Closer pickings could be had at Archer and Kedzie Avenues, an intersection that featured a retail assortment, including the Archer Big Store, and was populated with teenaged girls sporting slim, penciled eyebrows and babushkas firmly tied under their chins.

Archer Avenue, which cuts through the Southwest Side and continues on an angle all the way to Joliet, was originally Archer Road, an Indian trail beginning at 19th and State Streets. Its diagonal course resulted in lots of five- and six-way intersections, many with charming corner buildings that from a distance look as though you could clamp your fingers around them.

The street's main feature was its fast commute to the Loop, where early McKinley Parkers found additional employment opportunities. The plethora of downtown office buildings required clerical workers, mostly female, to process the paper end of their businesses and uniformed operators, mostly male, to run elevators not yet automated.

Shopping in downtown Chicago still held mass appeal in the fifties, an atmosphere of safe excitement, in which stores remained open on Mondays and Thursdays until 8:30 p.m. Modest budgets might have allowed a pair of glasses for $7.00 at Busch's Modern Optical, or a winter coat for the clearance price of $19.90 at Maurice L. Rothschild Company at State Street and Jackson Boulevard. Those willing to splurge for dinner could have Chinese, still cheap in those days, at South Pacific, downstairs at 30 West Randolph Street, or they could feign extravagance at one of Tad's steak houses, whose flaming grills could be viewed from the street. White-clad cooks broiled tough New York strip steaks, which could be had, accompanied by a small overdone baked potato and a partially wilted salad, for a buck-twenty-nine. McKinley Park's proximity and easy access could have residents home at a reasonable hour to accommodate work or school the next day.

Sunday was still reserved for rest and devotion. McKinley Park Lutherans attended St. Andrew at 37th and Honore Streets, featuring its own small bowling alley open to the public, and the German St. Philippus that later became United Church of Christ.

Catholics were divided among three parishes—St. Peter and Paul at 39th and Paulina Streets, Our Lady of Good Counsel, housed in an octagon building and holding heavily attended summer carnivals, and St. Maurice, at 36th Street and Hoyne Avenue. St. Maurice was pastored by Father Dominic A. Diederich and his assistant Father George Schomburg, who in many cases was friend and counselor to the parish faithful.

The huge park constituting the community's southern boundary, previously the Brighton Park Race Track, boasted the city's largest tennis club and a swimming pool. Kids swarmed the park in summer, taking part in craft classes or other organized activities or playing their favorite game, "piggy-move-up," on its baseball diamond.

Although the park's land was once owned by Chicago's sixteenth Mayor, six-foot-six Long John Wentworth, it was named after our 25th President, William McKinley. A statue of the fallen leader (assassinated in 1901) stands proudly at its northwestern entrance at 35th Street, where it intersects with Archer and Western Avenues. Also standing at this junction is Lindy's, famous for its chili and hamburgers and where many of the neighborhood kids dined on fries and cokes bought at the order window before walking home from the park.

A small town within a big city, McKinley Park was an enclave of safety and camaraderie and mutual concern by adults for each other's children. Kids wore hand-me-downs from neighbors and attended each others' graduations and birthday parties. While the proliferation of white flight to purported suburban havens of safety and affluence proceeded rapidly from many of the city's neighborhoods, McKinley Park held its ground and in some adept manner kept outsiders away far after others had succumbed to the panic of block busting. It was a community whose fragile sense of well being and safety was about to be shattered.

The Disappearance

"If you are good Presley fans, you'll go home and ease your mother's worries."

> Public appeal issued by Elvis Presley to Barbara and Patricia Grimes after their disappearance.

December 28, 1956, was a customary winter day in Chicago—coal dust in the air, dirty snow underfoot—but with the lingering celebratory spirit of Christmas. The temperature had reached a high of 36 degrees, not as bitter as Chicago could be, but weather reports promised deteriorating conditions.

For Barbara and Patricia Grimes, the time was special for another reason—Elvis Presley's premier movie, *Love Me Tender,* had completed its downtown run and arrived at their neighborhood theater, the Brighton, at 4223 South Archer Avenue. The theater was a short ride for the two girls on the #62 bus, once they walked the two blocks to Archer Avenue from their home at 3634 South Damen Avenue.

Like many teenage girls of the era, Barbara and Patricia were enthralled with Presley, so much so that they had joined his fan club and were awaiting their membership confirmations. By the time *Love Me Tender* began its Brighton Theater run on December 28th, the two smitten fans had reportedly seen the film and witnessed the cinematic demise of the Presley character Clint Reno ten times. In real life they would precede their handsome singing idol in death by twenty years.

Barbara Jeanne Grimes and Patricia Kathlene Grimes were born on May 5, 1941, and December 31, 1943, respectively. Their parents, Joseph Cornelius Grimes and Lorretta Marcella Hayes Grimes had been married on July 21, 1924, when. Joseph was barely seventeen and ten months younger than his bride. Their first child, Shirley, was born in 1926, followed by Leona in 1928. The couple, whose children would eventually number seven, separated when the youngest was an infant, leaving the weight of the day-to-day parenting responsibilities on Lorretta's shoulders.

In the terms of their uncomplicated divorce, filed in 1951 and finalized on December 17th of that year, Joseph Grimes was ordered to pay $150.00 attorney fees and $35.00 a week in child support for the two girls and their three siblings who still lived at home. This was a substantial chunk of his weekly $70.00 or $80.00 earnings as a truck driver for Bozzy Cartage at 3724 South Washtenaw Avenue. At the time of his daughters' viewing of the Presley film on December 28, 1956, Joseph was living in a large yellow brick apartment building at 2738 West 61st Street with his second wife, Grace Wrage Grimes. The couple had married on August 18, 1956.

Lorretta Grimes worked long hours as a file clerk at Parke-Davis Pharmaceutical, 130 North Franklin Street, but the family was reportedly on welfare for part of the children's early lives—often without heat and lights. When not working, Lorretta could sometimes be seen sitting outside watching her kids play. She once stated that what the family lacked in money, they made up for in love.

Patricia Grimes, spunky, with an impish smile, planned to celebrate turning thirteen with several girlfriends, who'd been invited to attend a small party at the Grimes home on Saturday night, two days earlier than her actual birthday. She was in seventh grade at the parish school, St. Maurice, at 36th Street and Hoyne Avenue, right around the corner from their house.

Barbara, smaller by three inches and slightly more subdued, had attended all eight years of grade school at St. Maurice and was a sophomore at Kelly Public High School.[5] To help out at home she worked

---

[5] Kelly High School still stands at 4136 South California Avenue.

part-time at Wolf Furniture House on Archer Avenue[6]. The two sisters, seemingly inseparable, often walked about hand in hand.

At around 6:20 on December 28th, the two girls began dinner consisting of tuna fish—fare common for Catholics on Fridays in those days—and white and sweet potatoes, mashed together—"…everything I like," Barbara commented to her mother as she sat down to eat, "and I'm hungry." It was during dinner that she brought up the movie. "Mama," she began, "can we go to the show tonight?" She was intent upon going to the neighborhood opening of the movie, patting her mother on the shoulder as she begged for permission. Concerned about the worsening weather descending upon the city, Mrs. Grimes tried to convince her insistent child, who had been taking medicine for a cough, that going out was a bad idea. Eventually she conceded, with the stipulation, based on safety concerns, that "Petey," as the younger girl was known, accompany her. She gave Barbara $2.50, instructing her to put the fifty cents in the zipper of her wallet, to save for carfare home.[7] The two sisters ate Dolly Madison chocolate chip cookies for dessert and at 7:15 kissed their mother good-bye and left for the theater.

---

[6] This address, 4211 South Archer Avenue, is now Watra Church Goods Store.
[7] CTA charged a mere 25 cents for a bus, trolley, or el ride in 1956.

Lorretta Grimes expected her daughters home at 11:45, which would have allowed them two viewings of the movie, but she was already feeling uneasy by 11:30, as though she sensed something was wrong. At midnight, she sent another daughter, Theresa, 17, and 14-year-old son Joey to the bus stop at 35th Street and Hoyne Avenue to watch for them. After three buses failed to yield their sisters, they returned home, and their mother called police.

At 12:30 a.m., Officer Herman Steinberg of the 20th District, Brighton Park Station, met Joey and Theresa at Archer and Damen Avenues. Joey reiterated to Officer Steinberg that his sisters were missing. Steinberg took a description of the girls and alerted all officers in the district on the midnight patrol. About 2:05 a.m. Mrs. Grimes called the squad room and again reported the disappearance. Her daughters had attended a movie, she told the officer answering the phone. She described them, and message 5428 was sent out.

The next day, juvenile officers, policewomen, and District 20 detectives began an investigation. By Monday, which was New Year's Eve and Patricia's thirteenth birthday, Chicago newspapers were carrying stories of the girls' disappearance, and police were setting up a special task force to locate them. They canvassed door-to-door and searched alleys, garages, outbuildings, and basements in the area bounded by 51st Street, the drainage canal, the Chicago River, and Laramie Avenue. Railroad detectives joined in a search of the Sante Fe railroad yards, based on the idea that the girls might have locked themselves inside one of the freight cars. Police sent circulars to all precincts throughout the city, as well as law enforcement agencies all over the United States.

As the search intensified, Barbara and Patricia were, it seemed, simultaneously everywhere and nowhere.

Sightings

"They were alone and looked happy."

> Statement to police by Dorothy Weinert, friend and classmate of Barbara Grimes, who sat with her and Patricia in the Brighton Theater the night they disappeared.

"My sister and I hadn't planned to see the movie with them," Dorothy Weinert DeSaga says today, "we just ran into them at the concession stand, so we all sat together."

DeSaga says that she left the theater after the first viewing of the Presley movie, because her six-year-old sister, Jeanette, had fallen asleep. "I told Barbara and Patricia that I would like to stay but that I needed to get Jeanette home, and we left. We caught a bus right away and were home in ten minutes. The next morning Joey Grimes was pounding on our door, yelling, 'Did you see my sisters?'"

Police had no reason to doubt DeSaga's claim that she and her sister had joined Barbara and Patricia in the Brighton Theater, so their attendance at *Love Me Tender* was considered an indisputable occurrence. Subsequent reports of sightings, which poured in almost daily while police searched for the two girls, were not so definite and covered a wide range of locations and times of day and night.

CTA driver Joseph Smok thought they left his bus at Archer and Western avenues at 11:05. While this would have been the correct route for the girls, this intersection was several blocks west of their home and would have been a premature exit point. Smok believed he heard the two teens say that they were hoping to catch the oncoming northbound Western Avenue trolley, an incorrect direction if they were headed home.

Jack Franklin, a 68-year-old northwest side security guard, offered directions to two girls he would later identify as Barbara and Patricia. He passed them near Lawrence and Central Park avenues on the morning of December 29th, less than twelve hours after they left the theater. He remembered the two teenagers by their rudeness. They were wondering aloud where to catch a bus, and when he pointed out the stop, one of them snapped, "Shut up." The location of that sighting was near the last place that three murdered boys, Anton and John Schuessler and Bobby Peterson, were last seen alive fifteen months earlier.

Judy Burrow, 15, a friend of Barbara Grimes, reported to police captain John McCarthy of Brighton Park that she had seen the sisters at

2:30 p.m. the same day, walking west on Archer Avenue, two blocks west of Damen Avenue at Hamilton Street.

Patricia's classmate Catherine Borak, eating at Angelos, a McKinley Park restaurant at 3551 South Archer Avenue, thought she saw the younger sister walk past the establishment's window at 6:30 that evening with two girls she didn't know.

A cashier at the Clark Theater at 11 North Clark Street reported that he saw the girls there at 12:45 a.m. on Sunday, December 30th.

A North Shore motorman, Bernard Norton, thought two girls who boarded his train in Waukegan that afternoon, were the Grimes sisters. The Edison Court station, where Norton noticed the girls, was just two stops north of Great Lakes Naval Training Center. It seemed like a meaningful tip. Police had been searching for two sailors known only as Terry and Larry. The girls had reportedly met the two servicemen downtown at the Oriental Theater in November[8] and at some point brought them home, where Lorretta Grimes served them coffee and cake. Mrs. Grimes recalled that their last telephone contact with the girls occurred on November 28th.

---

[8] Elvis Presley's first movie *Love Me Tender* was showing at the Oriental Theater in late November 1956.

While the world around her cheered in the new year, Mrs. Grimes held a quiet vigil in the living room of her small, two-story brick house, unable to eat or sleep, and continued reports of sightings produced spurts of hope followed by disillusionment. On January 1st, her two missing daughters were allegedly seen again on the city's transportation system. Bus driver Robert Curran from Cicero identified them as passengers on his Damen Avenue route.

During the following week several people in Englewood reported seeing them. George Pople,[9] a 36-year-old night clerk at Unity Hotel, 750 West 61st Place, said two girls fitting the descriptions of Barbara and Patricia requested a room on either December 29th or 30th—he couldn't remember which of the two nights—at around 9:00. All forty-two rooms on the second-floor workingmen's hotel were full at the time, but Pople stated that he would have refused them anyway, because they were so young.

Again, the girls' association with the two sailors came up, when three Kresge[10] employees at 63rd and Halsted Streets insisted that they

---

[9] Newspaper accounts were inconsistent concerning the name of this witness, which vacillated between "Pople" and "Pope."
[10] Long-time Chicagoans might remember the now defunct Kresge "five and dime stores" located at various sites throughout the city. This one was located in the Englewood Shopping Center, a popular retail mall among Southwest Siders.

saw the girls spinning Elvis 45 RPMs[11] on the store player on January 3rd with two men in Navy uniforms. Lt. Donald Keevers, a Chicago policeman, described one informant's description and account as "most convincing." Lt. Keevers' son, Tom, remembers a few visitors to the Keevers' household, reporting sightings that were not so convincing. "Once a woman came to our door and said she'd seen the girls in the bark of a tree," he recalls, "but my dad was always polite."

Sometime during those first few days in January, an unidentified phone caller told Theresa Grimes that her sisters' bodies had been placed in garbage cans behind the Brighton, prompting a police search of the alley behind the theater, which yielded nothing.

On January 5th, police administered a lie detector test to Southwest Sider Leona Marlow, an eighteen-year-old girl who initially reported that she saw the two sisters after they disappeared. She later claimed that she had actually seen them before December 28th. Her test was inconclusive.

A junk dealer in western Iroquois County, Illinois, about ninety miles south of Chicago, said that, on the morning of January 5th, he saw

---

[11] 45RPMs, for those too young to remember, were the mode of recording popular music, introduced in 1949—a round, black vinyl disk, 6 3/4 inches in diameter, with a 1 1/2-inch hole in the center that fit over the turntable spindle. There was a song on each side.

two young teen girls with two men in the town of Gilman, Illinois, in a maroon 1947 car with Tennessee license plates and a Chicago vehicle sticker.

At this point, police captain John McCarthy said he believed the two girls were still in the area close to home. Mrs. Grimes concurred. On January 6th, after attending Mass at St. Maurice and reacting with sorrow to the absence of her girls in the choir, she reiterated her view that they would not be away on their own. "I don't think my girls have run away. If there was any way for them to get home, I know they would. They are not the type of girls to run away."

She pointed out that on the night of December 28th, Barbara had surrendered her paycheck of $20.25 and a Christmas bonus of $5.00 from her part-time job at Wolf Furniture to aid in covering the family's household expenses. "Does that sound like a girl who is going to run away?" she asked police. She showed reporters identical gifts her daughters had received for Christmas—portable radios in leather cases. "If they had wanted to go away, they would have taken these," she insisted.

On January 10th, switchboard operator Henrietta Marshall received a phone call at Catholic Youth Organization headquarters at 1122 South Wabash Avenue, prompting a search by police of hundreds of automobiles in the Illinois Central Railroad's 12th Street Station and the underground Grant Park parking lot. "For God's sake, I need help," the young caller first told Mrs. Marshall, "I want to talk to a priest." When Mrs. Marshall told him there was no priest available, he asked her if she knew the location of the Grant Central Station parking lot. Mrs. Marshall said she did not. "Well, I've got a thirteen-year-old girl tied up in the trunk of my car there," the young man said, before hanging up abruptly. Police found no one at the reported site—dead or alive.

Later in the month, two perplexing occurrences, one bordering on the occult, intensified the mystery. Wallace and Ann Tollstan, whose daughter, Sandra, was a classmate of Patricia Grimes, received two phone calls around midnight on January 14th. The first call woke Mr. Tollstan, who hung up when no one spoke. Mrs. Tollstan answered a second call fifteen minutes later and heard a voice ask, "Is that you, Sandra? Is Sandra there?" Before they could awaken Sandra, the caller hung up. Mrs. Tollstan was convinced that the voice, which she described as frightened and depressed, had been that of Patricia Grimes.

On January 15th, switchboard operator Ann Dorigan received a bizarre phone call at the central police complaint room at 1121 South State Street. A man declining to identify himself insisted that "those two missing girls" were dead and could be found in Sante Fe Park at 91st Street and Wolf Road near the Sanitary Ship Canal. The park was a picnic area located in the village of Tiedsville, where stock car and motorcycle races were held, an area frequented, according to police, by young men with flattop haircuts and long sideburns. The caller informed Mrs. Dorigan that his revelation had come from a dream.

Police searched the park and found nothing. They were able to trace the call to a pay phone at Green's Liquor Market at 6108 South Halsted Street and discovered that it had been made by Walter Kranz, a 53-year-old steamfitter for the railroad, who lived in a boardinghouse at 5949 South Halsted Street. Kranz, uncommonly tall and gaunt and of uncertain mental state, was brought in for questioning and released.

The *Chicago Sun-Times* headline on Thursday, January 17th, read, "Identify Lost Sisters as Dixie Job-hunters." Pearl Neville, a 54-year-old traveler, was making her way from Nashville, Tennessee, to her home in St. Paul, Minnesota. During a stopover in the Greyhound Bus Station at Randolph and Clark Streets, she noticed a newspaper item about two missing girls. Upon viewing their published photos, she believed them to be the two "tired, bedraggled" girls she'd met in a Nashville bus station rest room on January 9th.

"I matched the names quickly, because I remembered that 'Grimes' fitted them well," the woman told police, "they looked quite 'grimy' when I saw them." She said that the three had spoken briefly, then gone to a state employment agency together to apply for work.

A clerk at the agency in question remembered the two girls and identified them by their pictures as having applied there on January 9th, under the Grimes name. A lieutenant in the special investigation unit in Chicago stated that the clerk's memory of the names was more important than her identification of the photos; unfortunately, records were not kept for transient applicants. The traveling witness, usually referred to in newspaper accounts as "Miss" Neville but once referred to as a widow, was pictured in the *Sun-Times* meeting with Mrs. Grimes, who reacted to her claims with disbelief laced with hope—disbelief that her girls would run away and hope that they were alive.

The Nashville report spawned suspicion that Barbara and Patricia might have headed south to see Elvis Presley. "We haven't seen those girls yet," declared Joe Gagliano, an inspector for the police department in Memphis, which was Presley's home town, "but it wouldn't surprise me if they showed up." Gagliano told a *Chicago Daily News* reporter that such missions were common practice among Presley's underage fans and that during the previous month as many as fifty runaways seeking a glimpse of the singer had been located and returned to their parents. "We pick them up, put 'em in a squad and drive them once around Presley's estate," Gagliano told reporters. "Then we put 'em on a bus for home."

It was following Miss Neville's alleged sighting that the king himself released his press statement, admonishing the girls to return to their worried mother. Mrs. Grimes, convinced that her daughters were being held somewhere against their will, also made a public appeal. "If whoever took my girls will just let them go," she pleaded into a TV camera, "I'll forgive them from the bottom of my heart."

Her appeal fell on deaf ears, as false and mysterious phone reports persisted. A young girl who failed to identify herself told the distraught mother that two men who'd offered her a ride to a Stickney dance claimed that they'd taken "the missing girls" dancing at a place near 50th and Laramie Streets in that suburb on Tuesday, January 15th.

Mrs. Grimes had interrupted her agonizing living room watch on January 12th to take a late night train ride to Milwaukee. She'd been escorted on the trip by FBI agents, in response to a series of ransom letters, later found to have come from an institutionalized mental patient. One of the letters instructed her to sit in a downtown Catholic church with $1,000 on the pew beside her. It cruelly promised that Barbara Grimes would walk in and retrieve the money, deliver it to him at some point nearby, then return with Patricia.

It's likely that, as Mrs. Grimes sat waiting and praying, her two lost daughters already lay lifeless under a pile of snow on a remote roadside closer to home.

The End of the Search

No. 31116. Cancel missing message No. 54428. Barbara and Patricia Grimes, 3634 S. Damen, Bodies now at the County morgue (Captain) McCarthy, 20 (district) Jan. 23, 1145.

> Message delivered by police teletype, January 23, 1957.

On Tuesday, January 22, 1957, 39-year-old construction worker Leonard Prescott was driving east on German Church Road. Prescott was minding his own business, which, on that afternoon, was food shopping in nearby Willow Springs. The time was one o'clock.

"I didn't have a care in the world," Prescott would say later. "My wife told me to go out and get groceries. I was going mighty slow and I noticed these flesh-colored things underneath the railing." Prescott was referring to a metal guardrail that lined the bridge over Devil's Creek, a tributary of Flag Creek, about two hundred yards east of DuPage County Line Road. From his car he could see under and beyond the railing, on a flat piece of ground that extended for only about ten feet, after which it sloped steeply to the creek bed below. He stopped but didn't get out of the car at that point.

Prescott wasn't sure what he saw but had a feeling it was something troublesome. He and his wife Marie had noticed newspaper stories about two missing Chicago girls, but he failed to make the connection. Thinking he needed to consult with someone, he sped home to tell Marie, showing up at the door in a state of agitation.

"My God, I can't believe what I just saw," he exclaimed. "You've got to come with me and look." Marie, who worked as a punch press operator by night and cared for their five children—including a pre-schooler crippled with polio—by day, wasn't too thrilled by the prospect of leaving the house just to look at something. "You're crazy; you're seeing things," she chided her husband, "I've got to get ready for work tonight."

But something in his urgent manner told her to oblige, so she tied a babushka over the curlers in her hair and went with him. "We didn't want to get too close," Mrs. Prescott said in 2002, remembering the horror of that moment long ago and how she and her husband never moved closer than fifteen feet from the stark white objects—objects that Mr. Prescott initially thought might be store mannequins, but which were, in fact, the frozen bodies of Barbara and Patricia Grimes. Once they'd driven to the spot and she'd made the horrific confirmation, he had to carry her back to the car.

The stunned couple then raced to the Willow Springs police department, less than a mile away, where they encountered Sergeant John Alexander McKay, a two-year veteran, arriving at the station. Sergeant McKay would later testify at the inquest:

I was just going to get out of the car, when this man, Leonard Prescott, came alongside. He was all excited, said he'd seen two dummies lying alongside the road on German Church Road along County Line Road. I told him that I would immediately go over there, and he should show me the spot. When I got near there he stayed about fifteen feet from the line of the incline. I went down and I noticed the bodies behind the guardrail alongside of a ravine. I climbed out and looked over the ravine and I seen that there were two nude girls, I guess about thirteen or fifteen years of age, somewhere around there.

McKay immediately got into his car and phoned the sheriff's police and gave them the information, then stood by until the proper authorities arrived to take over.

Just who the proper authorities were would soon come under question, but police from various departments—county, city, and nearby suburbs—rapidly converged on the scene, creating a sea of fedoras atop grim faces. Sheriff Joseph Lohman, square-shouldered, full-featured, and normally possessing a pleasant smile, immediately took charge. Lohman, by all accounts a decent man, was an academic with aspirations to the governor's mansion and totally out of his element in police work. He would be assisted in this investigation by Undersheriff Thomas Brennan and Harry L. Glos, aggressive assistant to Coroner Walter E. McCarron.

The father of the victims, Joseph Grimes, dressed in his work clothes and flanked by two policemen, was led to the site to make a positive identification. The two officers had met Mr. Grimes at Bozzy Cartage Trucking Company, where he worked as a driver, to tell him of the discovery and ask him to look at the bodies. Bracing himself for the ordeal, he was offered more time to prepare for the worst possibility, but he expressed a desire to proceed. "Yes, they are my daughters," he stated afterward, before he slumped and burst into tears.

Barbara Grimes lay on her left side, her legs drawn up slightly. Her head was covered by the body of her sister, who lay on her back with her head turned severely to the right. They wore no clothing. Lohman, Brennan, and Glos initially agreed that the bodies had lain on the roadside several days, hidden by the heavy snowfall of January 9th and preserved by the frigid temperatures that plummeted to zero on the night of January 10th. Sheriff Lohman ordered tarpaulins to cover the area, already disturbed and trampled, while more than 150 policemen scoured the area for clues.

Lohman, Brennan, and Glos found themselves in a gruesome de javu. It had been only fifteen months since they had gathered at the shocking death site of three boys from the Northwest Side, brothers Anton and John Schuessler and their friend Bobby Peterson. Lohman immediately noted "the extraordinary parallel" between the murders, pointing out the most obvious similarities. "In both cases," he was quoted, "the murderer was careful to remove every piece of clothing. In each case the bodies were similarly disposed of."

Accordingly, the boys, about the same ages as the two sisters, had looked like mannequins when first viewed by an unwary route salesman, who had stopped to eat lunch in Robinson Woods Forest Preserve. Fifty-five-year-old Victor Livingston had been an extra in Hollywood movies in the 1930s, but on October 18, 1955, the happily married, tee-totaling liquor salesman certainly expected no further fanfare from life when he drove his car into the parking lot at the edge of the woods off of Lawrence Avenue. He turned to retrieve his lunch bag from the rear seat and spotted the boys stacked like fire wood in an adjacent ditch.

Just as the Grimes sisters had attended a movie on the date they disappeared, the three boys had set out for a Loop theater to see *The African Lion*. The death sites of both the boys and the Grimes sisters were, although many miles from each other, in close proximity to the Des Plaines River.

There was one major difference. It had been obvious from the start that the boys had been beaten and had died of strangulation. No such clarity existed in this new murder. There were superficial puncture wounds in Patricia's chest that police speculated were made by an ice pick or similar object, bruises on Barbara's face, and loss of skin tissue on both girls due to rodent activity. There were no clear signs of injuries that could have been fatal—no bullet or stab wounds, no strangulation marks, and no apparent head trauma. What actually killed Barbara and Patricia would have to be determined by modern technology, such as existed in the 1950s.

Their bodies were moved, by order of Harry Glos, to the Cook County Morgue to await autopsies, while the search for their clothing and other evidence continued, hindered by a new snowfall.

A City Traumatized

"Yokels that would do that are not fit to live."

> Shop teacher at Kelly High
> School upon hearing of the
> discovery of the Grimes
> sisters' bodies.

Shock and anguish permeated the scene at 3634 South Damen Avenue, as friends, neighbors, and clergy gathered to offer solace and support to the Grimes family. It was inconceivable that death would visit them again. The couple's second eldest child, Leona Freck, who had married and left home, died at Holy Cross Hospital on August 8, 1954, at age 26, after a prolonged illness.

"We lost Leona, my second eldest daughter, two years ago, after she underwent a kidney operation," Mrs. Grimes told reporters. "All of us were with her while she was in the hospital and we knew she had the best of care before she died."

Once Barbara and Patricia disappeared, Mrs. Grimes feared she would lose them as well, and she seemed to assume some personal responsibility. One day while the girls were missing, she appeared at the

St. Maurice convent door. Bursting into tears, she related to one of the nuns her decision to allow Barbara to leave the house on the evening of December 28th, only if accompanied by her sister—ironically—so that they'd be safe. "Now, I've probably lost them both," she cried.

On Tuesday, January 22nd, her worst fears were realized. Authorities had alerted her earlier in the day that two female bodies had been discovered southwest of the city, and she instinctively knew they were her daughters. "They [the police] wouldn't believe me," she cried, upon hearing the news, still convinced that the disappearance of her girls had not been taken seriously enough by police. "I want to go to church," she murmured repeatedly, then headed toward St. Maurice. On her way, longtime neighbor Mrs. Joseph Kozak intercepted her and led her to the Kozak residence at 3630 South Damen Avenue. Mrs. Kozak then called Father Schomburg, who came immediately and accompanied Mrs. Grimes back to her home, in time for the awful confirmation her ex-husband Joseph Grimes brought from the death site. "It was them," he announced, ending her sleepless, 26-day vigil on the living room sofa.

The two afternoon dailies caught the story before they went to press. The *Chicago American* reported on the nude bodies of two girls *believed* to be the missing Grimes sisters. According to an informant, "The girls seem to be about fifteen years old. In general description and size they appear to resemble descriptions of the Grimes sisters." The *Daily News*, whose headlines read, "Find Bodies by Road," reported positively that they were Barbara and Patricia.

The following day the two morning papers, the *Chicago Daily Tribune* and the *Chicago Sun-Times*, blasted the headlines. Princess Caroline of Monaco had been born at 3:27 a.m. Chicago time, but the long-awaited news occupied lower positions on the pages. It was hard to even notice Monaco's happy birth announcement, wedged between pictures of the smiling, sweet-faced victims and weeping family members. Immediately upon identifying the girls Mr. Grimes had been photographed, supported and led away from the scene by the two solicitous police officers, his face a tearful grimace. Mrs. Grimes, shown with her fists clenched, crying and looking devastated, was quoted as wishing her life could have been taken and her girls allowed to live.

Wednesday morning, at St. Maurice School, students lined up in eerie silence. "It was as though a pall had been dropped over them," commented one teacher, adding, "No one thought of murder when they disappeared." The principal, Sister Ritella, who had known Barbara when she attended St. Maurice, described both girls as average students who were totally devoted to their mother and to their home. Teachers at Kelly High, the school attended by Barbara Grimes, expressed the same shock and sadness.

Reporters contacted Dorothy Peterson and Eleanor Schuessler Kujawa, mothers of the three murdered boys, for their reactions to the news. Mrs. Malcolm Peterson, mother of Robert, stated that she was almost too shocked to comment. "I'm just so taken aback," she managed, "I really can't say anything. It's just terrible. Part of your heart is gone...I know how Mrs. Grimes must feel and I know God will watch over her."

Mrs. Kujawa, recently remarried after her first husband, Anton, died one month following the murders of their two sons, sent Mrs. Grimes a sympathy card with a personal message:

My heart goes out to you, Mrs. Grimes, for I know the terrible experience you have been through. Only a mother knows the worst, and although I hoped for the best, I, too, knew the day my children disappeared, that I would never again see them alive. Have courage in God and pray the killers of your daughters will be brought to justice.

The widespread sympathy for the bereaved family was expressed in the form of food delivered by neighbors to the Grimes home and cards and letters, often containing donations to help them with their living expenses, since Mrs. Grimes had not worked for weeks. A man Mrs. Grimes didn't know brought her $2.00, claiming the amount had been slated for an upcoming bowling game. A group of neighborhood teenage girls rang doorbells asking for donations and raised $253.00. Children unacquainted with the family took it upon themselves to raise money by gathering donations from their friends. Seward School first-grader David Powers collected $6.08. A neighbor brought $25.00 to the Grimes home, impressed that fourteen-year-old Joseph Grimes had shoveled her sidewalk every day, including the Tuesday he learned about the death of his sisters.

Back of the Yards Neighborhood Council set up a fund and received donations by mail, varying in amounts from fifty-cent pieces to a check for $500.00. The council, founded in 1939 and the oldest community organization in the United States, established a fund drive, headed by retired police captain Matthew Murphy and Father Schomburg from St. Maurice. Mrs. Grimes used money from that fund to outfit herself and her kids for the funeral services, which, it was announced, would be conducted free of charge by Wollschlager Funeral Home.

At one of the stores where Mrs. Grimes shopped for clothing, a clerk who identified herself as a widow with a nine-room home, offered to house the Grimes children. St. Maurice Church, where the funerals were to take place, provided gravesites for the girls.

While the outpouring of sympathy and support couldn't bring her children back, Mrs. Grimes found comfort in the fact that people cared. She was shown in the Saturday, January 26th *Sun-Times* newspaper, attempting to hold her emotions at bay as she set fire to her $7,726.25 mortgage.

The wake for the two girls had begun on Friday, January 25th, and on Saturday, it seemed that half the city turned out. A nun from St. Maurice convent said she came out of her door and saw people lined up all the way from the entrance of Wollschlager Funeral Home to Archer Avenue. Perhaps it was curiosity, a taste for the morbid, or an urge to connect and express their sympathy and outrage that brought so many spectators to the tiny funeral home to view the two closed caskets with their occupants' photos on top.

Whatever the motives, the Grimes case was a citywide preoccupation. People still unsettled by the killing of the three boys, people who had searched, prayed, and hoped for a happy ending to the disappearance of the two girls, were stunned again by this double murder, and panic about the safety of children reigned with new intensity. Parents recoiled in fear, keeping youngsters inside and in view as never before.

Many felt compelled to help solve the crime. The Back of the Yards Neighborhood Council, in addition to their efforts to defray the expenses of the Grimes family, distributed letters to area residents offering a $1,000 reward for information leading to a conviction in the case and outlined ways in which the public could assist.

Friends Danielle Blotteaux, and Barbara Drzewiecki, both seventeen, who matched Barbara and Patricia in size and stature, posed in clothing duplicating what they wore the night they disappeared. The photographs were published in the newspapers, with the hope the pictures would jog the memory of anyone who might have seen the Grimes sisters.

Some became unwitting players in a drama that would forever mark their psyches.

Classmate Rosemarie Rancatore Eggers was a pallbearer for Barbara, although they were barely acquainted. She learned of the disappearance on the radio during Christmas vacation.

"It sent chills down my back," she says today, "but I never thought in a million years how serious this was and that they would find the girls dead." Once they were found, Eggers remembers having to open the locker for detectives and finding Barbara's course book with a failing grade that she had not taken home to her mother.

Eggers also never dreamed what she might be getting herself into when she called Mrs. Grimes during the disappearance to express her concern and ask if Barbara and her sister had been found. "A squad of police, like ants, converged on my home," she remembers. "They flooded through the house, filled the back yard and alley; they seemed to be everywhere at once." She was terrified when a policewoman came toward her out of nowhere and said, "Come with me, dear, if you have anything to tell me," and ushered her into their unoccupied dining room, where she fired questions that the frightened, bewildered teen had no idea how to answer. The police then followed her everywhere. They took her out of class and appeared at her home at night, despite her insistence that she had shared only a gym locker with Barbara at Kelly High School and otherwise knew nothing.

Because of her scant association with Barbara, she'd been surprised when a priest from St. Maurice Church had called and asked her to serve as a pallbearer. She describes the funeral as a three-ring circus that nearly made her sick. "The press were the worst," she says, "stepping all over headstones, plants, and flowers. It was awful."

The press, it would soon become clear, were not the worst. All too often after such events, a small number of demented souls find delight in acting on their fiendish tendencies. Someone, having seen the pallbearers' names and addresses listed in the newspapers, had warned their already distressed parents anonymously by telephone that they, too, would never see their daughters again. Eggers remembers hearing from a detective that the calls had been made and that they would all have to go home. "I was afraid for my mom," she says today.

Dorothy Weinert DeSaga was also a pallbearer for Barbara. "My mother got a call from someone who told her, 'Your daughter's next,'" she says. "I remember the police coming to the cemetery and driving me home."

Rosemarie and Dorothy and the other stunned, unwary girls had carried their friends Barbara and Patricia to their graves at Holy Sepulchre Cemetery in Worth, Illinois, where they were laid to rest near the grave of their sister Leona, the mystery surrounding their deaths widening with each passing day.

So stressful was pressure on St. Maurice clergy—the shock and fear among parishioners, the intense public attention, and endless police presence—that the Chicago Archdiocese saw fit to whisk the pastor and his assistant off to Florida for separate week-long vacations.

The Investigation

"We're not going to repeat some of the mistakes we made the last time."

> Statement by Lt. Joseph Morris of the Chicago police unit, head of the investigation of the Schuessler and Peterson murders.

D espite the best intentions and efforts of police and officials from various jurisdictions, the investigation into the murders of Barbara and Patricia Grimes was flawed from the beginning.

Ironically, the discovery of their bodies occurred one day after civic leaders offered a $100,000.00 reward for the solution of the Schuessler-Peterson murders fifteen months earlier. The reward was set as a first undertaking of the newly established Crime Detection Institute. The formation of the institute, the brainchild of Judge Julius Miner, was prompted by the failure of police to solve the triple murder. With Henry

Crown, Chicago philanthropist and civic and business leader as chairman and Judge Miner as president, the group now considered a second reward.

Police had been harshly criticized for their handling of the Schuessler-Peterson investigation, which so far had produced no resolution and appeared to be driven by political rivalries and personality clashes. And, just as in that case, the multi-jurisdictional feature of this new double murder would hamper this investigation, which was further compromised by the destruction of clues by incautious reporters and photographers anxious to tell the story.

An assumption that the bodies of the girls had lain there the entire twenty-six days they were missing evoked the obvious question: Why had no one seen them?

Mrs. Elizabeth Lundeen, who lived on Sixth Avenue in LaGrange, told police she'd driven to a friend's house around noon on January 22nd—at about ten miles an hour because of the snowy conditions—and passed right by the spot on the bridge. "I'm sure the bodies weren't there then," she insisted. American Airlines pilot P. Marvin Althaus, who lived within feet of the scene, drove across the bridge at 8:30 that morning and likewise saw nothing.

Mr. and Mrs. Peter Wootos lived on German Church Road in 1957. "When the bodies were found, we were shopping in LaGrange," Mrs. Wootos says today, "and we saw the news clip on a television set in the store. On our way home, we saw all the police cars."

She remembers that Breaker, their Great Dane, was determined to run across the road that day, something he'd never shown an interest in doing before. "It was as though he sensed something," she says. Her husband, who passed away in 2002 at age 90, said to her, once they discovered what was happening, "Now I know why Breaker was awake and whimpering all night." Curiously, although the behavior of their dog might have created the impression that something untoward was occurring on the bridge over Devil's Creek during the night of January 21st, Mr. and Mrs. Wootos were never questioned by police.

Officials and the public in general awaited the autopsies with great eagerness, certain that they would jumpstart an investigation woefully deficient in clues and information. Coroner Walter McCarron was attending the Eisenhower inauguration in Washington, D.C., and, in his absence, assignment of the procedures was left to his assistant, Harry Glos. Glos demanded to be present, as a representative of law enforcement agencies, during the five-hour examination performed by three esteemed pathologists—Drs. Augustus C. Webb of the coroner's staff, Edwin F. Hirsch of St. Luke's Hospital, in charge of the histologic[12] portion of the examination, and Jerry J. Kearns, chief pathologist of St. Elizabeth's Hospital and former pathologist for the coroner's office. The heavily credentialed Dr. Walter J. R. Camp, considered one of the top toxicologists in the country at the time,[13] tested blood and tissues taken from the bodies.

Surprisingly, initial results from the autopsies yielded no positive information. Dr. Kearns referred to the postmortem examinations as "one of the roughest cases I've seen during my many years in the coroner's office." The *Chicago Tribune* headline, on Thursday, January 24th, read "Autopsy Widens Mystery." The report on Patricia, signed by Drs. Hirsch, Kearns, and Webb, stated:

Patricia Grimes came to her death because of secondary shock resulting from exposure to temperatures that reduced her body temperature

---

[12] Histology is the microscopic study of structures taken from vital organs.
[13] Dr. Camp was professor of toxicology and pharmacology at the University of Illinois College of Medicine and Secretary-Treasurer of the American Academy of Forensic Science.

below the critical level compatible with life, that is, to systemic hypothermia. The statement was repeated with regard to Barbara.

The unanimous determination by Drs. Hirsch, Kearns, and Webb that the girls died by freezing was reached by an elimination of definite causes, such as shooting, stabbing, strangling, or monoxide poisoning. The puncture wounds in Patricia's chest, they determined, occurred after death and were not serious enough to have been fatal, and other injuries were from rodent bites, also post-death.

"The murderer in this case," said Dr. Kearns, "was diabolically clever. He used a method we are unable to detect. Perhaps he is a person trained in chemistry and with a knowledge of unusual poisons." Determining exactly what "mysterious agent" killed the sisters, he indicated, might take weeks. A time of death, pending studies of the stomach contents of the older girl, could not be established.

The first suspect in the case was Walter Kranz, who had called police on January 15th and claimed that the girls were dead and could be found in Sante Fe Park. Once the bodies had been discovered within two miles of that location, police re-arrested Kranz, described by the newspapers as an enigma, and held him at the Englewood station for observation, questioning, and lie detector tests regarding his dire telephone prediction.

According to records at the Chicago and Northwestern Railway, where Kranz had been employed since June 1956, the six-foot-five "little giant" was absent from work four times between December 28th and his second arrest. Kranz blamed the absences on the illness of his wife. He received high praise from his boss, who described him as a good worker who knew his trade. Kranz, who described his statement as merely a "hunch" that occurred to him after a night of drinking, vehemently denied any connection to the murders.

"My soul is clear," he stated.

Police had a second matter to question Kranz about. Handwriting experts were fairly certain that he'd written a letter to Mrs. Grimes before the bodies were found, demanding that $5,000.00 be left in a locker in the LaSalle Street Railroad Station. Police never found enough evidence to hold Kranz beyond their interrogation.

By Thursday, January 24th, police were questioning another suspect, whose arrest and detention would mark the beginning of an investigative debacle that would dazzle, confuse, and anger the public, while adding to the family's grief.

Bennie Bedwell

"I don't know why he's lying, but he's a liar, liar, liar. Only God knows the truth."

> Mrs. Lorretta Grimes, denying that her slain daughters would have caroused with Bennie Bedwell on Madison Street.

The term *skid row* originated in the Seattle, Washington, area. In the 1800s, it was applied to a strip of saloons, gambling houses, and dilapidated hotels on the thoroughfare where lumberjacks wet logs, froze them to make them slippery, and slid them downhill to the sawmills. Over the years the name was applied to other urban areas populated by people who were, ironically, unemployed or underemployed, and who were given to less-than-wholesome lifestyles. This population grew after World War I and during the depression of the 1930s, then dropped during the government programs of the 1940s and the country's subsequent spurt of prosperity.

In 1957, the skid row population of Chicago on West Madison Street was estimated at 12,000.[14] The area wasn't terribly far from the neighborhood Barbara and Patricia Grimes called home, but the disposition of its inhabitants[15] made the idea of two Catholic girls of such tender ages spending time there implausible to the public and unbearable for the family.[16]

Cab driver Reno Voldis Echols, in response to photographs published in the newspapers, came forward and told police that he'd seen the Grimes sisters on the morning of December 30th in the D & L Restaurant at 1340 West Madison Street. Echols, who lived less than a block from the Skid Row establishment, insisted that the two girls were there at 5:00 a.m. with two men—one he didn't recognize and one with sideburns like Elvis Presley whom he'd seen there before.

His story would be corroborated by the restaurant's elderly owners John and Minnie Duros. They both identified the two girls as the slain

---

[14] This, according to Thomas J. Young in Chapter 14 of *Alcoholism & Substance Abuse in Special Populations*, 1989.

[15] While Skid Row was a haven of seedy hotels, dingy bars, and an assortment of unemployed and sporadically employed persons of less-than-sterling character and limited ambition, one West Side resident wrote a letter to the editor of a Chicago newspaper reminding readers that interspersed and surrounding addresses were inhabited by upstanding, working family people.

[16] The publicity focused on Skid Row during the investigation of the Grimes case prompted police sweeps of its various bars, checking ages of patrons and issuing citations against hotels where "repeated immoral acts" had taken place.

sisters and the man with the sideburns as a patron they had employed sporadically at the D & L to wash dishes in exchange for meals.

Mrs. Duros described a scene she initially said took place in her restaurant early on the morning of December 30th. She said that two teenage girls, one taller than the other, entered the restaurant with the dishwasher and another man and sat in a booth.

The taller girl was so sick or drunk she was staggering. They [the two couples] sat in the booth for a while listening to Elvis Presley songs on the jukebox, then they went outside. The taller girl came back in and sat in the booth and put her head on the table. She said they [the two men] wanted her to get into a car but she didn't want to. The men and the other girl came back in, and I told them to let that girl alone—she's sick.

Mrs. Duros was distracted by customers, one of whom was Reno Echols, in the front of the restaurant, and while she attended to them the man she identified as Bedwell half dragged the older girl out the back door, while the younger girl protested.

According to Mr. Duros, the group returned later in the morning, and it appeared that Barbara had paired off with the Elvis look-alike.

"They were carrying on and I asked them to leave," Duros said. "He paid the bill and they left." Duros went on to say that their on-and-off employee returned to the restaurant several days later, and when Duros asked what happened to the girls, he answered, "We got 'em." Duros warned him, "You'd better send those girls home, because the police are searching for them. It'll be your neck if they catch you with them." With that, Duros finished, the man hung his head and left.

There were a number of witnesses claiming to have seen the girls around the Madison Street area at various times on December 30th. Willie Jackson, 217 South Paulina Street, saw two girls walking with a man near Madison Street and Western Avenue at 3:30 a.m. Vito Martinez, 25, of 325 Lexington Street, said he saw the Grimes sisters a half hour later at 4:00 a.m. at Madison Street and California Avenue. Another witness believed he saw them in the evening around nine o'clock. Walter Scott, who lived at 1845 West Madison Street, told police he saw them at 3:00 a.m. at Madison Street and Ogden Avenue and then at the D & L Restaurant later that morning.

However, Minnie Duros would later be called into the Monroe Street station for a chat with detectives concerning a discrepancy in the dates of this alleged visit to the D & L by the missing sisters. The restaurateur seemed unsure at times if the Sunday morning in question was December 30th, as she had originally stated, or January 6th, one week later.[17] Detectives would also want to know why she had waited so long to report seeing the foursome, since police had searched the Skid Row area while the girls were missing. One of their stops was the D & L, claimed detectives Sidney Rubin and Henry Ulrich, but Mrs. Duros would deny having been questioned during that time. She would bristle when asked why she hadn't been concerned about the young ages of the girls. "I'm running a business and can't get involved in the affairs of my patrons," she would say defensively, adding that she hadn't really noticed how young they were, a statement in direct contradiction to her detailed narrative.

Sheriff's police located the unwary suspect at the Star-Garter Theater,[18] 815 West Madison Street, a former burlesque house that opened at 8:00 a.m. and showed double feature movies throughout the day and evening. He was taken into custody Wednesday, January 23rd, at 9:15 p.m., as he sat watching one of the two 1930s features of the day—*20,000 Years in Sing Sing* and *Roaring 20s*. Sheriff Lohman held him overnight

---

[17] The newspapers eventually began reporting the date as January 6th.

[18] The Star-Garter was once owned by Chicago Gangster Willie Bioff, who operated as a labor leader in the movie production business, extorting millions of dollars from movie studios by threatening work stoppages. He was murdered in Los Angeles in 1955 in his own driveway, when his car was blown up by a dynamite bomb wired to the starter.

for questioning without notifying other investigative agencies. The news broke the next day; January 24th headlines suggested that a West Side Romeo was being held under suspicion. From that day forward his name was a household word in Chicago.

The man in question was Edward Lee Bedwell, better known by his childhood nickname "Bennie." Tall, southern, and sporting Presley-like ducktails, Bedwell was born in Graves County, Kentucky. Although Bedwell's birth certificate states that he was born on March 4, 1936, the date recorded on every other document tracking his life events (with the exception of his marriage license) was one year earlier, March 4, 1935.[19]

While Bedwell was a young child, the family moved to Paris, Tennessee, the seat of Henry County, about 119 miles west of Nashville. The town, which, in 1957, had a population of about 9,000 residents, was located on the west branch of the Sandy River. It was named for Paris, France, in honor of Lafayette, who visited Tennessee in the early 1800s.

At his newly established age of eighteen and assigned Social Security number, obtained in Florida in 1954, Bedwell went to work for

---

[19] This includes his service records, his death certificate, and an application for a Social Security number, which he filled out on December 29, 1953, in Sarasota, Florida. According to one newspaper report, Bennie's mother stated that he was twenty at the time of the crime, while Bennie stated that he was twenty-one. Bedwell might have falsified his year of birth on the application in order to obtain work prior to his legal age of eighteen.

Barnum and Bailey and Ringling Brothers Circus in Sarasota, Florida, and then as a roustabout for a carnival in DeLand. At some point before arriving in Chicago, he reportedly was arrested for vagrancy in Las Vegas, Nevada.

Once in the windy city, Bedwell signed up for the United States Air Force at the induction center at 615 West Van Buren Street on December 14, 1954, and served less than six months. There are conflicting stories about his discharge, based in one version, on the tenderness of his hands, which had been burned when he fell against a stove when he was a year old. The second version involved a fracture of the kneecap, reportedly sustained in a laundry room brawl during his stint in the service. In another account, both incidences occurred; he fell and fractured his kneecap and couldn't use crutches because of tender hands. Doctors at Park Air Force Base Hospital in California performed skin grafts to no avail, and he was released April 4, 1955.

Bedwell's official birth date would have made him a scant twenty years old when sheriff's police arrested him on Skid Row for questioning in the Grimes case. He'd been living at the McCoy Hotel, a 70-cent-a-night flophouse in the infamous near West Side district, known for sleazy bars and hotels and their mostly indolent guests. He was the product of a broken marriage, and like his mother before him, he'd been propelled into adulthood early in life.

Ethel Lee Barnes was just sixteen when she became the fifth bride of John Edward Bedwell, thirty years her senior, on November 18, 1929, in his home town of Murray, Kentucky. Her complaint for divorce from Bedwell, granted on November 15, 1951, was based on grounds that he "willfully and maliciously deserted her," and during the last years of their marriage, "took to strong drink." He paid no attention, she complained further, to their two sons, whom she referred to as "Johnnie and Bennett." She described the boys as "grown and making their own way," although, on the day of the decree, Bennie was fifteen and his older brother, John Edward, born in 1930, was four days shy of his twenty-first birthday.

Mrs. Bedwell had remarried and with her new husband, Curtis Bradberry, a sewer repairman and older by sixteen years, occupied several addresses on Chicago's near West Side, beginning in 1951. By the time Mrs. Bradberry's younger son had gained notoriety as a Skid Row bum possibly facing a murder rap, she and her husband and their daughter Shirley lived in a ground level, three-room apartment in a graystone building turned rooming house at 1430 West Monroe Street.

Mrs. Bradberry, just over five feet tall and close to two hundred pounds, retained her Tennessee drawl as she described her son to reporters first as a lazy boy who thought the world owed him a living, then defended him in the next breath. "He's a good boy," she declared, "I'd like to go and see him. If he did anything wrong, I know he'd tell his mother."

Unaware of the trouble her younger son was in until she heard it from a *Daily News* reporter, she explained that Bennie had lived with her and his stepfather for a short time in November 1956, sponging small amounts of cash from them now and then for cigarettes and carfare, until she ordered him to leave. "My husband works hard for his money," she said, yet declared Bennie incapable of the brutality perpetrated against the Grimes sisters. "He never done that," she stated to reporters, adding a final, determined, "No."

A False Resolution

"He tells an evasive, disjointed, ambiguous, and disconnected story."

> Sheriff Joseph Lohman, following his initial 12-hour questioning session with Skid Row suspect Bennie Bedwell.

Chicago's hope for a speedy solution to the latest astonishing crime against two of its children rapidly built momentum. It then gradually waned and died, as its residents read daily news accounts of the investigative roller coaster ride that followed the arrest of Bennie Bedwell. "I'm sure glad Sheriff Lohman told me what I done," said the seemingly bewildered suspect the day after he was plucked from the anonymous coziness of the West Side theater.

"I was with the tall one," he told police, contradicting Duros' statement that Barbara and Bedwell were paired off. "She said her name was Carol." He further explained that, while they all attended a movie at the Century Theater at 1421 West Madison Street, the girls went to the rest room and ditched him and the other man by slipping past them in the lobby and exiting onto the street. "That's the last I saw either of them," he claimed, reiterating that they were not the Grimes sisters.

By the time police caught up with Richard Whittemire, the alleged second man at the D & L, Sheriff Lohman considered Bedwell a prime suspect. Whittemire, 28, confirmed his visit to the D & L with Bedwell in late December, minus any female accompaniment, but stated that he too was fuzzy on the exact date and that another man, dark-complexioned, probably Puerto Rican, was with them.

Whittemire, five-foot six and slight, had taken up residence in the Balboa Hotel in Cicero. No stranger to police interrogations, he had a record beginning in his home town of Mansfield, Ohio, as a juvenile delinquent and as a parole violator in 1951. On June 21, 1955, he was charged in Jonesboro, Arkansas, with grand larceny after stealing two watches valued at a total of $81.00. The same month, domestic troubles earned Whittemire another warrant, charging him with "willfully and feloniously" abandoning his pregnant wife Sadie Belle Whittemire on May 28th. In default of his bond of $500.00, he was sent to jail.

Whittemire described Bedwell as a ladies' man and denied joining him in any "amorous excursions" on West Madison Street. During his questioning by police, two girls came forward to corroborate Bedwell's story. Irene Dean, a nineteen-year-old Native American hitchhiker from Grand Rapids, Michigan, told police that she and her cousin, Carol King, 18, had been the two female companions of Bedwell and the other man. She claimed to have paired off with the second man, somewhere around the 29th or 30th of December, while Dean had been Bedwell's date. Mrs. Duros remembered seeing Dean in the D & L at other times, but without Bedwell.

No sooner had the two young women come forward, possibly clearing the erstwhile dishwasher of suspicion, than he made his first confession—not that he killed the Grimes sisters; rather, he repeated his earlier account of the drinking spree, replacing the characters of Dean and King with Barbara and Patricia.

He claimed he'd met them and a man already in their company at 7:30 or 8:30 a.m. on December 29th, a Saturday, at the Harold Club at Madison and Loomis Streets. (This would have placed the Grimes sisters on Skid Row less than twelve hours after they disappeared.) He offered the "biggest one" a drink, and she accepted, but when they attempted to order drinks for the four of them, the bartender refused to serve the girls due to their ages. They moved the party a few doors away to the Green Front Tavern, where they had six to eight rounds before heading to the D

& L for food, then back to the Green Front for more drinking. At their next stop, another tavern on Madison Street whose name Bedwell couldn't remember, they were told by the bartender that they'd had enough. They then proceeded to Ralph's Club, where they drank more, then on to the theater, where the girls supposedly disappeared from the lobby. Bedwell insisted that at the time he didn't know they were the two missing sisters.

In contrast to his earlier statement about the two cousins, that he hadn't see them again after they exited the theater, Bedwell claimed to have seen the Grimes girls again during the next few days, following their night of drinking, in various places around the area. He said that he saw the taller girl alone on two occasions and the two of them together at the Jackpot Tavern in the 900 block of West Madison Street. He claimed that on each occasion they refused to speak to him.

Meanwhile, police received information about a whole new batch of sightings. A few hours before Bedwell inserted the Grimes sisters into his story, Mrs. Marion Scaperdine, 2048 West 51st Street, told police that she had seen two men, Bedwell and a curly-haired second man, with the Grimes sisters at 4:30 on the afternoon of December 29th, just one day after they disappeared. Identifying Bedwell and the girls from photos, she said they were in front of a store in the 1900 block of West 51st Street, and that she had noticed them because the two girls appeared dazed. She also said that she saw a ballerina slipper on the curb across the street from her home the following day. Despite the low temperature and Barbara's cold, both girls had worn ballerina-type shoes to the Brighton Theater on December 28th.

Grace Kritikos, 50, manager of the New Albany Hotel at 231 South Halsted Street, claimed that she refused to rent a room to Bedwell, two girls, and a dark-complexioned man, the night Barbara and Patricia disappeared, because the girls were so young. After the bodies were found and the story broke, she contacted police and relayed the incident to them, making positive identifications of Bedwell and the two sisters.

Ann Povich, 39, a waitress at Mount Pindos Restaurant, 4950 South Pulaski Road, claimed that Bedwell was there with another man and two girls at 7:30 p.m. on December 28th. She said the girls had ice cream sundaes and that the men who left with them were Bedwell and another stocky, dark-haired man in a Navy coat. Although she identified the girls as Barbara and Patricia—even noticed that one girl called the other "Petey," which was Patricia's rather unusual nickname—she was likely mistaken, since the girls had left home at 7:15 on that night and were later seen in the Brighton Theater. Yet, Ms. Povich, who has since died, was adamant, and even in 1992, still found the experience almost too disturbing to discuss. "I tried to help the police back when the whole thing happened," she stated, "and they wouldn't listen to me."

Leonard Wass, 42, said two girls and two men—one a sailor—drove into the gas station he operated at 45th Street and Archer Avenue sometime during the first week of January. He remembered that the girls asked to use the washroom, and as they were leaving, the one he identified as Barbara gave him a strange look, one he interpreted as a desire to not get back into the car.

Edward Martel, 65, night clerk at a hotel at 1521 West Warren Boulevard, identified Barbara Grimes as the girl he saw leaving a restaurant at 1520 West Madison Street on January 5th. Robert Hilpertshauser, manager of the American Theater at 8 North Ashland Avenue, said he saw the girls there on various days between January 5th and January 10th.

Casey Jarzen, owner of a drive-in restaurant at 5444 Harlem Avenue, Stickney, agreed with his wife, Mary, his daughter, Donna, and their cook, Chester Wiziecki, that Bedwell and a second, dark-complexioned man were in the restaurant on January 11th with two girls they all identified as Barbara and Patricia. Wiziecki said that one of the girls was wearing a jacket with the name "Pat" stitched onto the front.

Pawnshop clerk Edward Frankel reported that a girl he thought resembled Patricia Grimes came into his shop at 950 West Madison Street early in January, hoping to pawn a watch. "I wouldn't accept it, because she was so young," Frankel told police. He recalled the encounter when he noticed the newspaper photo of the watch Barbara was wearing when the girls disappeared, "...a Bulova of a design you don't see very often," according to Frankel. "I remember it well."

Before the city could digest the latest headlines, Bedwell created new ones—that he had actually observed the murders of Barbara and Patricia at the hands of "Frank and Louie," two men who were carousing with the girls on January 13th. Frank was fair complexioned, he said, and Louie was dark, possibly Puerto Rican, and they were both in their twenties. He joined the two men and the girls and visited a few taverns on Skid Row before the entire party rode in a car to the southwestern part of Cook County. After stopping at a gas station at 87th Street and Archer Avenue, where the girls went to the washroom, they drove to the entrance of a forest preserve with a hilly incline and parked the car. Bedwell said that he sat in the front drinking, while the two couples made out in the back seat. He soon heard scuffling and turned around, only to see that the girls appeared to be dead.

He quoted one of the men: "We've got to do something about this. Everybody's got to keep quiet about it." The two men threw the girls' bodies out onto the side of the road and kept their clothes in the car, as they drove back to the city and dropped Bedwell at his hotel.

No one at the filling station remembered seeing the group that night, and no sooner had Bedwell pointed out the forest preserve entrance with the hilly area he had described, than he announced that he had made up the entire story. When asked why he had done so, Bedwell replied, "I thought you would let me go if I told you."

Having said that, the seemingly befuddled suspect further changed his story into a full-fledged admission of guilt, by replacing the Louie character with himself. He and Frank, he confessed, took the girls, on January 13th, to German Church Road, stopping along the way at Sunny Lane Restaurant at 5444 South Harlem Avenue, for hot dogs. He was taken by the sheriff, surrounded by police, reporters, and a crowd of curiosity seekers, for a demonstration of the activities of that night, in which he and his supposed accomplice each punched one of the two victims, rendering them both unconscious, and tossed them out into the snow.

At the spot where the bodies were found, he looked around, seemingly confused. "Yeah, this is the place," he said hesitantly. "I hit Patricia on the chin and I knocked her out," he told Lohman, "and how Frank knocked her [Barbara] out, I don't know." Appearing sorry for what he had done, he said, "I didn't mean to hit her so hard," and insisted that he hadn't believed the girls were dead when the two men drove away. At another point during the confession, Bedwell expressed sympathy for the Grimes family and blamed his bad behavior on his deprived childhood. "If I had a decent break at home and got some education, I wouldn't have been a bum around flophouses."

The final installment of his trilogy was full of contradictions and unexplained factors, such as the puncture wounds in Patricia's chest and the absence of other critical signs of violence on the bodies. Nonetheless, Bennie Bedwell was at last charged with the murders of Barbara and Patricia Grimes, and everyone, especially Sheriff Joseph Lohman, certain he had his man, breathed a sigh of relief.

To the Rescue

"This man has been without an attorney for five days."

> David E. Bradshaw, attorney
> for Bennie Bedwell

It is often said that prisons in America are filled with inmates who are there because they couldn't afford decent legal representation. In a case full of surprises, the otherwise down-on-his-luck Bennie Bedwell would not be included in that statistic. His mother, Mrs. Ethel Bradberry, had enlisted an up-and-coming attorney, David E. Bradshaw, to represent her son.

Bradshaw was a member of the Defense of Prisoners Committee, which was at that time a small group of private attorneys selected by judges to represent certain clients pro bono (possibly how Mrs. Bradberry acquired Bradshaw's services). The 1952 John Marshall Law School graduate, aggressive, a bit rough around the edges, would prove to be a daunting force against the determined sheriff.

"Here they present two young girls from a good South Side family, suddenly popping up on a wild spree on a skid row," Bradshaw said publicly, following his initial conference with his new client. Concerning the uneducated Bedwell, he continued, "The boy in the case is wholly illiterate, doesn't understand what is going on, and has found himself the main object in a case of nationwide interest."

Bradshaw went on to point the finger at Lohman and his investigative team for what he termed "unusual treatment" of his client, who'd been detained for five days. He suggested that the sheriff had conducted certain tests on Bedwell and that their results should be released. And, with that, the tall, square-shouldered ex-Marine was just warming up.

The sheriff's sigh of relief was a bit premature.

Lohman's neatly tied resolution of the murders evolved just days after the discovery of the bodies, but, just as quickly, it began to unravel. The unearthing of Bedwell's proclaimed partner in crime, William Cole Willingham, Jr., at the House of Corrections, where he was locked up on a drunk and disorderly charge, only added credence to Bedwell's original story—with some perplexing contradictions.

Offering to take a lie detector test, Willingham admitted that he'd been on a drinking spree with Bedwell with two young women. However, he insisted they were the two Indian cousins, Irene Dean and Carol King, from Petosky, Michigan, and not the Grimes sisters. Upon studying photos of Barbara and Patricia, he denied ever seeing them. Moreover, King, when shown photos of Bedwell and Willingham, identified them as the two men she and her cousin had met on West Madison Street and ditched at the Century Theater.

Willingham, born in Washington, D.C., and reared in Virginia, had been habitually in trouble with police. He said he'd last seen Bedwell on January 5th, the day they were carousing on Skid Row with the cousins from Michigan. He was arrested later that same day for being drunk and disorderly and was discharged from Holiday Court on January 6th. On January 10th, 11th, and 12th, Willingham claimed, he'd worked at Stineway Drug Store at 4761 North Broadway. As for the January 13th drive to German Church Road with the Grimes sisters, Willingham claimed to have spent much of that day around the Wilson Avenue-Broadway area, where he borrowed $1.00 from the cash register at the Stineway store and left an I.O.U. Willingham said he then went bar hopping until evening, when he traveled to the home of a friend who lived at 619 North Dearborn Street. Fred Pratt, manager at Stineway, confirmed both that Willingham had worked at the drug store on the 10th, 11th, and 12th, and that he had borrowed the dollar.

Witnesses further confused the issue by being divided on identification of Willingham. John and Minnie Duros insisted, from viewing his photo, that it was he who accompanied Bedwell and the Grimes sisters to their restaurant. Chester Wiziecki, cook at Sunny Lane, the restaurant where Bedwell claimed to have stopped for hot dogs on January 13th, was unable to pick Willingham out of a group of inmates. And, while Willingham denied that his nickname was "Frank," fellow inmates at the House of Corrections stated that he had indeed been called "Frank," because he liked to sing and fashioned his voice on Frank Sinatra.

To make matters even more baffling, police found a date book Willingham had been carrying, listing more than fifty female names. At the bottom of one page was a lone entry: "Grimes." Willingham passed the name off as a customer of his part-time work selling premium certificates for a photo studio.

Willingham is shown in the January 30th *Chicago Sun-Times*, confronting his accuser at the inquest for Barbara and Patricia, a contentious affair whose tone characterized the entire investigation. Added to the mix of warring officials was attorney Bradshaw, who entered each of the three post-mortem assemblies poised for battle.

A Turbulent Inquiry

"If there is anyone playing for the cameras, it is not I...."

> David E. Bradshaw, when accused by Coroner Walter McCarron of making a circus out of the Grimes inquest.

Coroner Walter McCarron began the first of three inquest proceedings by announcing that he believed all law enforcement agencies had cooperated with each other in the investigation. His first witness was Mrs. Grimes. A small, humble woman, not accustomed to the limelight or public forums, she was nonetheless prepared to serve as spokeswoman for the morality of her girls and to challenge the notion of their participation in Bedwell's debauchery. Equipped with eleven pointed questions and her own determination, she presented an impressive force for the room full of weighty officials to reckon with.

Shortly after McCarron began questioning her, Harry Glos broke in to instruct Bradshaw, on his feet, apparently to find a spot closer to the interview, to be seated.

"I would like to hear the testimony of Mrs. Grimes," Bradshaw explained.

That interchange prompted McCarron to address Bradshaw. "I want to be fair with you, sir, you are an attorney representing one of the people involved."

"One of the people involved?" Bradshaw repeated, then corrected the coroner. "I am the attorney of record for Edward Lee Bedwell." And when McCarron assured him that he had a right to hear everything, Bradshaw replied, "That is what I am trying to hear—everything—by moving up."

McCarron replied, "We have no secrets" and resumed questioning Mrs. Grimes concerning the last meal of Barbara and Patricia on December 28th. Bradshaw interrupted twice to say he could not hear and had McCarron repeat her last answers. He then informed McCarron that he had questions of his own to ask the witness, to which McCarron replied that he wanted to know what they were. Bradshaw said he preferred to question her directly. McCarron seemed intent upon protecting the bereaved mother from Bradshaw; yet, Bradshaw shared her agenda to vindicate Bedwell, albeit for different reasons. The exchange between

McCarron and Bradshaw was hostile. "You mean you want to hurt her some more? Go ahead," the angry coroner conceded.

"I am not here to hurt anyone," Bradshaw replied, "I am here to defend the rights of a boy."

Eventually, Bradshaw was granted his request and asked Mrs. Grimes her opinion concerning the presence of her daughters on West Madison Street and the guilt of Bennie Bedwell. His question, "Mrs. Grimes, as you sit there now, do you believe that Edward Lee Bedwell, who is here in this courtroom today, was involved in this occurrence with your daughters?" drew objections from both the coroner and Assistant States Attorney Robert J. Cooney.

Mr. Cooney:	That is very unfair.
Coroner:	Don't crowd that woman. How would she know who destroyed her children?
Mr. Bradshaw:	Mrs. Grimes seems to be willing to answer the question.
Coroner:	This woman is not on trial.
Mr. Bradshaw:	Now, Mr. McCarron, no one is trying to put this woman on trial.

Coroner:	How, in the name of God, would she know who destroyed her children?
Mr. Bradshaw:	I did not ask her that question.

Amid the bickering between Bradshaw and the officials, Mrs. Grimes did manage to reply categorically, "No," to both questions. When Bradshaw asked Theresa Grimes, the murdered girls' older sibling, if she believed the "alleged and purported" confession of Bedwell, she answered an emphatic, "No."

Cooney interjected, "I don't think the lady should be asked to answer whether that statement—," and Bradshaw interrupted, "She just answered it for the record."

Mr. Cooney moved that her answer be stricken on the grounds that "these people have had enough hardships without going into that."

Bradshaw rebuffed him soundly:

A legal objection is not founded on the fact that anyone has had a great deal of hardship. I am more than aware of the fact of the hardship that these people have had, are having now, and will have in the future. This is a coroner's inquest. It is the same thing as a preliminary hearing in felony court. The purpose of it is to determine whether there should be a bind-over to the grand jury...

Coroner's deputy C. F. Dore asked to address Bradshaw.

I want to inform you now that we are not governed by the rules of evidence here, and you are laboring under the theory that the coroner's jury is here to hold this man over to the grand jury. You are in error in your belief there...I may also tell you at this time that cross examination is not permitted at a coroner's inquest....

Bradshaw responded:

Mr. Deputy Coroner...I am not laboring under any false impressions as to the purpose of this coroner's jury. The question for them to determine is the true cause of death, but it is also to determine whether there should be a bind-over here.

Bradshaw engaged in a three-way clash when he questioned Sheriff Lohman about the location of Bedwell's confession. "Where was this purported statement taken, sir?" he asked. When Lohman answered, "a motel known as Caprello's at the corner of 55th and Cicero,"

Bradshaw, obviously trying to connect Lohman to Chicago's sinister gangster operations, asked him to name the owner.

The question drew an objection from Cooney. "It is irrelevant," he told the attorney. The three men went back and forth several times, Bradshaw insisting that the owner of the motel in question was a sheriff's deputy, Lohman dodging the question, and Cooney insisting that the matter was immaterial.

The sparring escalated in the final session on February 11th, when Bradshaw suggested that Richard Whittmire had been overlooked as a witness, and in their interchange, McCarron seemed to confuse Whittmire with William Willingham. Cooney pointed out that the people who had already testified as to the last time they'd seen the girls alive would help the jury determine the cause of death, which, he reminded Bradshaw, was the sole reason they were there. Bradshaw pointed out that the testimony of those interviewed had done nothing to help establish the cause of death; thus, why eliminate Whittemire as a witness for that reason?

A conflict of a different sort arose when the various officials questioned Dorothy Weinert about her meeting with Barbara and Patricia in the theater on December 28th. Dorothy claimed that she had seen the girls each buy a box of popcorn, and with that Mrs. Grimes jumped up and shouted, "Liar! You're a liar!" at the horrified girl, insisting that not only did they not eat popcorn as Dorothy testified, but that Dorothy hadn't seen them at all. The popcorn issue also created a discrepancy in the amount of money the girls would have been able to spend. Mrs. Grimes reiterated that she had given them $2.50, but forty cents carfare to the theater, admission of $1.50 for the two of them, and fifty cents for the two boxes of popcorn added up to $2.40, and according to Dorothy Weinert, they each bought a candy bar for fifteen cents, which brought the amount up to $2.70. A bus ride after the movie, if they took it, would have brought the amount to $3.10.

Mrs. Grimes would offend one other witness. Leonard Prescott was called upon to testify. Prescott became defensive when Bradshaw asked him about the position of the girls' bodies and quickly assured the attorney that he had not touched them.

"I did not say you did," replied Bradshaw.

Prescott said he thought he didn't have to answer the question, and when Bradshaw asked Cooney to direct Prescott to answer, Cooney concurred that he didn't have to and that they could discern the positions of the bodies by looking at a photograph held by Captain Fleming of the police department. "I think the best evidence is the picture of them,"

Cooney informed Bradshaw, who countered that Captain Fleming wasn't the witness he was questioning. Prescott never completed his answer, and a chart outlining the bodies was introduced.

Prescott was then dismissed, to his relief, but he and his wife Marie would be stunned and insulted when they both observed Mrs. Grimes, following his testimony, rolling her eyes as she remarked disparagingly regarding Prescott, "Boy, that one's a character."

"We were trying to help," Mrs. Prescott said of the incident, "and after all we were going through, we felt that she didn't have any reason to say a nasty thing like that about my husband."

The "all we were going through" to which Mrs. Prescott referred was the intrusion of police into their daily lives. "They kept showing up at our door early in the morning—six o'clock even," she recalled, "going through our cabinets and questioning us over and over, like they believed we had done something."

Such complaints about police behavior would soon surface. Bedwell recanted his confession, claiming police brutality; the toxicologists' ruling that the girls died December 28th (the night they disappeared) supported Bedwell's claim of innocence, and the police once again focused their investigation on the area surrounding the Grimes home

and the rural community where the girls were found.

Harry Glos

The sisters have just been placed in ambulance for transport to morgue.

Reporters and police gather at deadly scene on German Church Road.

Bedwell reenacting crime surrounded by Sheriff (to his right in dark coat) and reporters.

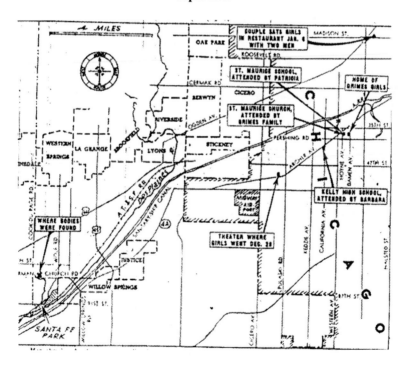

Chicago Daily Tribune map of pertinent locations in the case.

Patricia Grimes (age 12 on left) and Barbara Grimes (age 15 on the right).

An unsuspecting Barbara and Patricia celebrate Christmas with friends Dora Fisher (far right) and her sister Darlene (upper left), three days before they disappeared.

1400 block of West Monroe. Arrow indicates building where Bedwell visited his mother's rooming house apt. in 1957.

The Brighton Theater, closed and for sale, before reopening as an art center, then demolished in 2003.

Bennie Bedwell buried among fellow vets at Jefferson Barracks National Cemetery in St. Louis.

Barbara and Patricia Grimes share a headstone at Holy Sepulchre Cemetery.

Chicago Tribune picture of Mrs. Grimes awaiting news of missing daughters.

Skid row's McCoy Hotel, home of southern drifter Bennie Bedwell at time of crime.

Back to Square One

"I was a-scairt."

> Bennie Bedwell, claiming
> that abuse by police
> prompted his confession.

The determination by pathologists that Barbara and Patricia Grimes died December 28th, pretty much demolished Sheriff Lohman's case against Bennie Bedwell.

The absence of alcohol in the girls' systems eliminated the possibility that they were drinking heavily in Skid Row bars for days before they died. There was no food in Patricia's stomach, but examination of Barbara's stomach contents turned up particles of the fish and sweet potatoes she was known to have eaten before leaving home on December 28th.

Dr. Walter J. R. Camp concluded: "To suggest [that Barbara] received the same combination of food, in the same proportions, at the same interval before death, at another place, would be fantastic." Dr. Camp failed to find hot dogs in either of the girls' stomachs, discrediting Bedwell's statement that he and his male friend had bought hot dogs for the girls just before knocking them out and dumping them onto the side of German Church Road.

Findings by Dr. Camp and the other pathologists invalidated the fourteen-page confession by Edward Lee Bedwell, which he had retracted before Chief Justice Wilbert F. Crowley in Criminal Court. On a writ of habeas corpus, at a hearing beginning on January 30th and continued the next day, Bedwell said he'd resorted to the phony confession because police alternated between scaring him and bribing him. Chief Clifford J. Dreyer, Bedwell claimed, was the lead terrorist, who kicked him twice in the shins and slapped him, causing his lip to bleed. "He doubled up his fist," recalled Bedwell, "and there was a ring on his little finger. He hit me behind the left ear. Then he said, 'Now, let's have some answers.'" Walking toward the door to leave the room, Dreyer allegedly turned and told the terrified suspect, "I hope I've cooled down when I come back or else I'll have a blackjack with me. You wouldn't want me to work on you with a blackjack, would you?"

Bedwell also implicated a sergeant at the Bedford Park sheriff's police station, who forced him to strip to his shorts, socks, and shoes, and threatened to take him out to German Church Road where he'd be forced to walk around in a foot of snow. Lohman's Undersheriff Brennan, he claimed, gave him money for cigarettes after his first version of the story. Captain Fleming offered to give him a hand-me-down suit from his own closet if he would "be nice and tell the truth."

Sheriff Lohman admitted providing Bedwell with a jacket and a pair of boots, which he needed for the excursion to German Church Road for his reenactment in the cold, snowy weather.

Bedwell's memory served him well in concocting a story to satisfy his interrogators. One of his various jobs, which he'd held from around Christmas until January 23rd, was at Elegant Bakery, a bread shop located in the McCoy Hotel building at 949 West Madison Street, where he also lived. A co-worker read newspaper accounts aloud, providing details of the girls' disappearance and the discovery of their bodies, which he incorporated into his false confession. He also remembered the guardrail along German Church Road from a newspaper photo of the death site. Lohman, still convinced that Bedwell was guilty, denied the charges of abuse, adding that he'd become increasingly interested in "Willie" as an accomplice—referring to Bedwell's drinking buddy William Willingham.

Justice of the Peace Irving J. Eiserman refused bond, because the coroner's jury had not yet returned its verdict. On Saturday, February 2nd, Judge Crowley agreed that it would be possible for Bedwell to be released on $20,000.00 bond on the murder charge, if it could be shown that "proof was not evident nor resumption great" that he had murdered Barbara and Patricia Grimes. No bail could be granted if there was a clear-cut murder case against him.

Attorney Bradshaw had grilled Sheriff Lohman at that February 2nd hearing, pressuring him to admit that Bedwell lied when he confessed to the murders. He again brought up the location of the confession. Lohman, who, at times appeared angry by the line of questioning, maintained his composure nonetheless and offered this explanation: "Bennie did not want to be exposed to the photographers and newspaper reporters in the confusion attendant upon a station."

Assistant States Attorney Cooney questioned Bedwell about his charges of brutality and bribes, before members of Lohman's police staff took the stand and denied them. James Powers, a supervisor at Ajax Consolidated Company,[20] where Bedwell had worked for approximately a month, produced time cards documenting that he'd punched in at 4:19 p.m. on December 28th and punched out at 12:30 a.m. on December 29th, covering the time during which the girls disappeared.

---

[20] Ajax Consolidated Company, a small machine shop located in Cicero, manufactured, among other items, hand brakes for freight cars.

A co-worker at Ajax came forward and validated the alibi. Ralph Saylor, 26, worked the night shift at Ajax, beginning at 4:30 p.m. Saylor told police, who visited him at his home, that he'd clocked out at 12:30 a.m., December 29th, along with Bedwell. Saylor, now retired and living in Cicero, says he didn't really know Bedwell very well and assumed he was a daily laborer. Saylor remembers that night on the bus. "We rode down Cicero and transferred at Madison Street," he says. "I got off at Homan Avenue—I lived at 3338 West Adams Street—and Bedwell stayed on the bus, riding east." Judge Crowley continued the February 2nd writ of habeas corpus hearing until February 19th.

With Saylor's testimony, which promised to hammer the final nail in the coffin of Lohman's case against Bedwell, police went scurrying back to the neighborhood between the Grimes home and the Brighton Theater. Witnesses from the neighborhood gave persuasive statements indicating that the girls had proceeded on foot down Archer Avenue when they left the theater the night of December 28th and that they nearly made it home.

One was Roger L. Menard, who testified at the inquest. Menard, who lived with his parents at 3825 South California Avenue near Kelly High School, had turned nineteen on January 1st and worked at the downtown First National Bank of Chicago. He had attended *Love Me Tender* at the Brighton Theater the same night as Barbara and Patricia and had occupied a seat behind them and friends Dorothy and Jeanette Weinert.

After the Weinert girls left, the Grimes sisters caught Menard's attention. When the movie ended with the death of the character played by Presley, with its insert of him singing the title song, Barbara became emotional. "She cried rather hard," Menard testified, "as if her heart would break. Patricia didn't cry," he added, "but kind of, I would say, chided her sister because she was crying."

The girls left the theater about a minute after he did, Menard reported, walking behind him as he preceded east on Archer Avenue. He could hear them laughing. Just as they were walking past Fishman's Liquors, two doors east of Sacramento Avenue, he heard a screech of brakes and turned around and saw a late model green Buick pulling to the curb directly abreast of the girls. Menard explained his perception of the event. "The car came to almost a complete stop and I heard the motor racing as it pulled up, and the two sisters hesitated for only an instant, almost as if maybe they knew who it was in the car or maybe they just were surprised at the car pulling up, but there was a very slight, almost imperceptible hesitation, and the car pulled away and the girls kept on walking."

Just past 42nd Street, Menard stopped to look into the window of Lewis Men's Wear, and when he resumed walking, Barbara and Patricia were ahead of him, maybe a hundred feet. A second car, a black Mercury, occupied by two teenage boys, pulled up. "The one on the passenger side rolled down the window and said something to the girls," Menard told Coroner McCarron. "I wasn't close enough to catch exactly what was being said. They [the girls] looked at each other and they laughed or giggled to themselves, and they kept on walking, and the car pulled away."

Coroner McCarron then attempted to obtain as accurate a description of the car as possible. When asked how he recognized the year, Menard said, "I would say it was a '49 because it is a model car that a lot of teenagers buy because it's very easily customized." He believed it to be a four-door, jet black car, in excellent condition, and that it may have had a sunshield on it, also black, over the front windshield. As for distinguishing features of the two boys, Menard said that, despite light from the store windows, he couldn't be clear on their descriptions, except to say that the driver looked to be tall, and the other appeared short, because he was low in the seat.

Earl Zastro, 15, and Ed Lorden, 17, were riding around that night and observed the girls on the latter part of their journey. The two boys, who today are still friends, lived in the area and knew Barbara and Patricia, not personally, but by sight. At around 11:25, with Lorden driving, they noticed two girls making their way east on 35th Street between Seeley and Damen Avenues. "They were giggling and jumping out of doorways at each other," says Zastro. Curious as to who they were, the two boys drove around the block to get a better look. "Oh, yeah," one said to the other, "it's those two Grimes sisters."

Zastro had mentioned the incident a few days later to a policeman questioning patrons in Angelos' Restaurant, at 3551 South Archer Avenue, and nothing came of it—until police renewed their interest in the area in February. "They kept taking me out of school," Zastro says of police, whom he believes were desperate for a resolution. "First they'd threaten me, trying to get me to confess, then they'd give me treats."

Zastro lived with his parents above their grocery store at 3833 South Wolcott Avenue, where they also sold sandwiches at lunchtime to nearby office employees. "The police actually accused me of killing the girls and hiding their bodies in the store freezer," he says incredulously.

Zastro later joined the Air Force and was home on leave in the summer of 1959, when police resumed their interest in him. "They [the police] followed me around even then," he says. "They'd sit outside our house until I came out and trail me wherever I went. After that I served overseas for three years, and that ended it."

The description by Zastro and Lorden of the two sisters' playfulness as they approached Damen Avenue was music to their mother's ears. "That's the two of them," she said of her girls, "playing a game of hide and seek."

Free At Last

"It's costing me 500 bucks from my own pocket, but I think it's worth the money."

> Morris Brown, bondsman
> who procured $20,000.00 for
> Bennie Bedwell's release
> from jail.

For Bedwell, the county's accommodations were proving to be preferable to his digs on West Madison Street. Kept in isolation at the request of his attorney, he had music piped into his cell and dined on meals he noted were better fare than he could buy on his own. Monetary offers poured in from magazines and television shows anxious to "get the real story," and a theatrical agent had the bright idea that if the befuddled prisoner would learn to sing and play guitar he'd take him on tour, proclaiming him "the next Elvis." Locally, Bedwell enjoyed a minor following, with people writing to his attorney to determine what size clothing they might donate to the indigent prisoner. Some sent small cash contributions, eventually totaling close to $150.00. None of his newfound fans or wanna-be managers, however, was offering the $20,000.00 bond money required to set him free.

During his final days in jail, the investigation continued, and new leads—both on the Southwest Side and near the death site—made headlines, then fizzled. One report was that of Robert J. Mitchell, who owned and operated a combination grill and filling station at Joliet and Willow Spring Roads. Mitchell told a story of arriving at his station to open for business on the morning of January 19th and finding a twenty-something man there requesting a push for a stalled car. Mitchell obliged and drove him to German Church Road, in a tow truck, to a spot about four miles from the site where Barbara and Patricia were found. A second man about the same age was waiting there in a 1956 medium green, two-door Ford hardtop with elaborate bumper guards.

Mitchell noticed a section of gray cloth, which might have been a blanket or a coat protruding from the trunk of the Ford and asked the second man why he hadn't used it to keep warm during his wait. "They gave me a none-of-your-business look," Mitchell told police. "I was alone, so I didn't press the matter." Barbara Grimes had been wearing a coat matching the color of that cloth when she left home on December 28th. Mitchell was adamant that neither man was Bennie Bedwell.

Sheriff's deputies discovered hair and what appeared to be human flesh inside a corrugated cardboard box in the snow on German Church Road, just west of County Line Road, on the farm of Emmett Keller. The locks of hair were wrapped in September and November 1956 newspapers. Ultimately, the police crime lab determined that neither the flesh nor the hair were from the bodies of the girls.

Police found a message printed with chalk across a two-by-four wooden support on the back of a shack located near the death site, on a five-acre tract owned by Carl Rink, who lived in Clarendon Hills. The words, "HELP HELP B & B HELP HELP," were interspersed with one arrow pointing upward and one pointing downward, and the "L" and "P" on the first word were printed backwards. Lt. David Purtell, handwriting analyst, was enlisted to compare the writing on the board to the name, "ELVIS", printed on a stove in a gas station at 37th Street and Damen Avenue, purportedly by one of the Grimes sisters (this, according to station attendants). Purtell said that the single word contained too few letters to make a telling comparison.

Closer to home, local gang members were rounded up and questioned. Four of them had been arrested previously for the beatings of Kenneth and Robert Lenkart at 35th Street and Hamilton Avenue on

December 24th and of Gerald Gierut, a sailor on leave, in McKinley Park, just south of the Grimes home, on December 29th.

One of them was 18-year-old Richard Byrnes, of 3713 South Hermitage Avenue. Byrnes had been questioned by police on New Year's Eve, while the girls were missing, because he'd reportedly been seen talking to them. Claiming to know only Theresa Grimes, he insisted he hadn't seen her for several months. Another of the group, 18-year-old Robert Darding, reportedly the head of a gang, said he was also acquainted with Theresa and that she had accused him, on December 29th, of abducting her sisters from a restaurant at 35th and Wood streets. Police uncovered several incidents of assault by these boys but were unable to connect them with the double murder.

As police resumed house-to-house canvasses in the McKinley Park neighborhood, truck driver Daniel W. Eshelman came forward to report seeing the girls on the night of December 28th. Eshelman, employed by Standard Fuel and Furnace Oil Company, located at 430 West 37th Street, saw two girls he described as "bobby-soxers," wearing babushkas and resembling the Grimes sisters, get into a dark-colored car with three men as they stopped in front of his truck at Archer and Western Avenues. Before they entered the car, he said, a young blond man about twenty got out and spoke to them. One of the girls appeared to know the man, and the other stood away from the car, as though reluctant to speak with him. The car moved east on Archer Avenue, and Eshelman soon lost sight of it. Although he made the observation at about 10:45 the night of the disappearance, he waited until after the girls were found to report the incident, claiming that at the time he wasn't sure it was important. He also stated that he delayed telling police what he'd seen, hoping to spot the car again—perhaps to be the hero of the day or to be certain of his information.

On February 4th, a 1951 Mercury, hoped to be the mystery car that kept cropping up in witness statements, was found abandoned near McKinley Park. The car's owner, Charles Tirva, Jr., 28, who had served time for contributing to the delinquency of a minor and for burglary, turned himself in to police, who administered a lie detector test and found him to have no apparent knowledge of the murders.

Another truck driver, who owned a 1949 Mercury four-door sedan, was accused by four girls from Kelly High School, of indecent exposure. The students identified Joseph P. Dinstale, 27, of 2901 West 38th Street, as the man who made improper suggestions to them near 38th Street and

Kedzie Avenue late in January. He was administered a lie detector test and found to have no connection to the murders.

Police picked up Victor Snoklus, 18, of 821 West 31st Street, and three juveniles, supposedly identified by Patricia's friend Dora Fisher as youths who offered her and the two sisters a ride on December 27th. The boys were questioned and released.

Brothers Charles and David Bobb, 25 and 20 respectively, both of 1235 Chestnut Street, went to the Grimes home to report that they'd been incarcerated in Georgia and while there were told by a fellow arrestee that he was afraid his car—a Mercury, which he had abandoned in Detroit— might have been used to abduct the sisters.

Meanwhile, Mrs. Grimes received a phone call from a woman who claimed she saw a black Mercury at Taylor and Halsted Streets, occupied by two men with long sideburns. And, on February 8th, the ubiquitous Mercury showed up in a report from a Southwest Side resident, car salesman Stanley Zdziarski, 35, of 4002 South Archer Avenue. Zdziarski was watching television in his upstairs apartment the night of December 28th, when he heard voices outside. He went downstairs to the front door and saw a car parked at the curb. The men in the car were talking to two girls standing on the sidewalk. Zdziarski was able to describe one of the men as about six feet tall, 180 pounds, with blonde, bushy hair and wearing a beige Army battle jacket. One of the girls, he claimed, was dressed in a gray car coat and babushka, similar to those worn by Barbara Grimes. His description of the car closely matched Menard's—a black 1949 or 1950 Mercury. He couldn't say whether the girls got into the car or kept walking. He confirmed the date by checking the television guide for the movie he'd been watching.

That same day, police began a search for the author of two letters mailed to the Grimes home, one arriving a week previously and one on February 7th, implicating himself and someone named "Trudy" and beseeching forgiveness from Mrs. Grimes. Anonymous threats were mailed to her as well, prompting authorities to provide police protection both at their home and for individual family members as they went about their routines.

Separately, two letters from different men were mailed to Sheriff Lohman early in February, prompting his surreptitious flight to Alabama on February 6th to question their authors. A man in Athens, Alabama, claimed to know Bennie Bedwell. The second letter, mailed from Decatur, Alabama, mentioned a car possibly used in the abduction of the girls.

A third truck driver, out of town when he contacted a fellow driver who then contacted police, stated that he saw two girls near 71st Street and Manheim Road, less than three miles from the death site, walking in the dark at 12:30 a.m. on December 29th. He expressed certainty that the clothing the girls were wearing, clearly discernible in the scope of his headlights, was identical to that worn by Barbara and Patricia on the night of December 28th. He failed to report the sighting earlier because he was not aware of the murder until mid-February.

Police also revisited Leonard Prescott, who once again described driving down the road for some innocuous errand and noticing a discarded fruit basket about a mile northwest of the spot where he'd found the bodies. Prescott drove past the item, and once he'd arrived home, thought he might want to make use of it. With his ten-year-old son in the car, he drove back and picked it up, then discovered that it contained a wallet, which he turned over to police with the idea that it may have belonged to one of the girls. He was rewarded with a second lie detector test and additional questioning. Mrs. Grimes, when shown the wallet, stated that it did not belong to either of her daughters. The investigation was faltering on every front. There was desperation in the air.

The *Chicago Tribune,* in a questionable move, solicited opinions from its readership, paying $50 for each that was published. Letters poured in from far and wide at the rate of thousands every few days.

"The murder happened the night of December 28th," wrote James Mangan of Chicago. "They [the girls] were picked up by two or more young men, one of whom was a butcher's son or who had access to a place with a walk-in ice box…"

Mrs. Anne Apolskis of Gary, Indiana, wrote that the girls were killed by someone they knew or recognized after being invited for a ride home. "Being girls of good moral character," she presumed, "it would seem unlikely they would accept a ride unless they knew one or more of the occupants [of the car]." Mrs. Apolskis believed that there were three or four youths who'd been drinking and made improper advances toward the sisters, whom she believed threatened to report them to her mother. "Somewhere in Chicago," she concluded, "are three or four youths who are going through the motions of a normal everyday life with this terrible secret locked within them. They will find no peace unless they confess their crime."

Mrs. Harry Burkhart had a unique idea. She felt that the rodent bites on the bodies of the girls held the key to the investigation. "Most

...small rodents that frequent the fields and woods in the winter in Chicagoland are not necessarily carnivorous," she wrote, "so let's assume the rodents are rats." She proposed that the girls, while running in and out of doorways as they approached Damen Avenue the night they disappeared, as reported, might have encountered an unlocked door to an unheated building, locked themselves in, and frozen to death. "...perhaps a janitor or owner of the building enters and discovers the bodies....Terrified of becoming involved with the police, he decides to dispose of them." She suggested that police concentrate their investigation on unheated buildings.

D.C. Lewis of Chicago prefaced his theory with a denial of his own investigative proficiency. "Amateur detecting is not an avocation of mine," he began, then posed, "Could it not have been possible that two friends or acquaintances of the two girls picked them up with no ulterior purposes, merely to drive them home?" Lewis' question had been asked by many, but he then veered off the beaten path with an unusual idea that, in his mind, explained both the cause of death and the puncture wounds in Patricia's chest.

"That ...in some secluded spot, the girls were hypnotized and commanded to remove their clothes ...then demonstrated the subjects' immunity to pain by three pin pricks—then something went wrong…I would recommend a search be made among friends and acquaintances of the girls to find a boy, or boys, interested in hypnotism."

Donald E. Fernley, of St. Joseph, Michigan, believed that the same murderer killed the Grimes sisters and the Schuessler and Peterson boys, "someone suffering," he suggested, "from a persecution mania, stemming from a real or imaginary grievance or injustice done him by the police or other authorities." He made the unlikely comparison between them and a gangster slaying during the summer of 1955, perhaps referring to Charles Gioe, who was shot as he was about to drive away from a meeting with another mob associate, Hyman Wiseman. "The killer has a place of operation where the children were confined and where he was able to deal with them one at a time," Fernley wrote, suggesting that police search a point halfway between where the boys and the sisters were found. Mr. Fernley offered his $50 remuneration to the Grimes family.

It appeared that Bedwell had been omitted as a suspect in the minds of the public, but Sheriff Lohman remained steadfastly invested in his guilt, even as it became obvious that his star suspect would go free. Earlier in the month of February, he had taken one more potshot at Bedwell's alibi, by holding Richard Whittemire, Bedwell's drinking pal, in a West Side hotel for additional questioning about the night of December 28th. Whittemire had worked with Bedwell at Ajax Consolidated and, at some point in the investigation, had reportedly signed a statement that Bedwell had not shown up for work on December 28th. While Ralph Saylor to this day does not remember seeing Whittemire on the bus with Bedwell, Whittemire later stated that he had taken the bus to the West Madison Street area with Bedwell and that they had visited both the D & L Restaurant and a Skid Row tavern.

Back home in Tennessee, Bedwell had many Parisians on his side, including the mayor himself. Aaron Brown, Sr., had been a criminal lawyer in Paris for twenty years before being elected mayor. Brown traveled to Chicago with his wife and two sons, having been hired by Bedwell's family and friends to assist in his defense. Mayor Brown conveyed the support of his hometown folks and offered Bedwell free transportation back to Paris and a job there upon his release. "I feel that the boy, with this experience, is ready for a change," said Mayor Brown. "We used the occasion to take a family trip to Chicago," says his son, Aaron, Jr., also a criminal lawyer, who now lives in Oregon. "I remember staying at the Drake Hotel." Brown says his father, who died in Memphis,

Tennessee, on September 23, 1997, believed Bedwell was railroaded and did not commit the murders.

While the newly focused investigation, marked by empty leads and futile interrogations, was floundering, Bedwell was freed on $20,000 bail. Morris Brown, a bondsman from Champaign, Illinois (no relation to Mayor Brown of Bedwell's home town), professed a combined motive of altruism and a desire for publicity, when he took it upon himself to secure the bond money to facilitate Bedwell's discharge from jail. Brown, described by newspaper columnist Irv Kupcinet as a colorful character, initially offered his own building, located in Lovington, Illinois, and valued, according to his own estimate, at $70,000, as security. Brown claimed to have used the same building as security for a $50,000 bond for two men, former state auditor Orville E. Hodge and his administrative aide, Edward A. Epping, both serving prison terms.[21] When the building was rejected as worth only $6,800, Morris, whose slogan read, "You don't need the wings of an angel if you know Morris Brown," put up $500 of his own and enlisted the Summit Fidelity and Security Company, 1137 South

---

[21] Orville E. Hodge was state auditor from 1953 to 1956. He depleted the state budget, requiring emergency appropriations of over $500,000 to finish out his term, and embezzled more than a million dollars. He was indicted for conspiracy to embezzle state funds and misappropriation of bank funds and served fifteen years in prison. Epping, his hand in his boss' cookie jar, served time as well.

State Street, to secure the remainder of the $20,000 necessary for Bedwell's release. And, to ensure that Bedwell didn't abscond afterward, Brown assigned his six-foot-two, 235-pound nephew, Monte Goleman, to follow him around.

Bedwell's release was quite an event. Able to write only "Bennie Bedwell" and not his full name, "Edward Lee," the prisoner was granted special permission by Chief Justice Crowley to print the name instead. The ceremonious signing took place on February 5th, attended by Bedwell's attorney, who then whisked the smiling vagabond off in a pink Cadillac (possibly owned by Mayor Aaron Brown) to parts unknown. "Bennie is not going back to the flophouses and saloons," Bradshaw announced before their dramatic departure. He promised the finest care for the allegedly reformed drifter and a press conference later that day at the tony Belden Stratford Hotel, 2300 Lincoln Park West, for an eager media.

Imbroglio

"This may cost me my job."

> Harry Glos, regarding his
> public statement that the
> Grimes sisters did not die
> December 28th.

With the early February release of Bennie Bedwell from jail and his fate in the hands of the grand jury, one would think that the principals in the investigation could settle down and focus on chasing clues. Rather, it was the calm before the storm.

On February 14th, coroner's assistant Harry Glos resurrected the ostensibly settled issues of time and cause in the deaths of Barbara and Patricia. Glos, who shared Lohman's belief in Bedwell's guilt, shocked the city by announcing that the two girls could not have died the night they disappeared. He brought up the matter of the ice layers around their bodies, which proved that they were warm when left on German Church Road, and pointed out that only after January 7th would there have been enough snow to create the ice layer and conceal the bodies.

"The puncture wounds in Patricia's chest were never adequately explained or explored," he said at a Thursday evening, February 14th, news conference. He was convinced that not all of the damage on their faces was produced by rodent bites, that those and other signs of violence (including Patricia's three chest wounds) proved that they'd been beaten and tortured.

Glos had plenty to say about the content of the girls' stomachs, stating that he'd heard one of the doctors performing the autopsy say that curdled milk was found in Barbara's stomach, a finding not mentioned in the official report. Despite the strong denial and outburst of Mrs. Grimes at the inquest, Glos said that he believed the claim of Dorothy Weinert that both girls had eaten popcorn at the theater on December 28th and considered the fact that popcorn didn't turn up in the stomach contents further evidence that they didn't die that night.

Glos didn't stop there. He made public the findings reluctantly confirmed by the Chicago Police crime lab that Barbara Grimes had been sexually molested. Chicago police complained that Glos had undermined their efforts by revealing the molestation of the older girl, which they'd hoped to keep secret for use in questioning suspects. (According to a former Lohman staff member who observed the autopsy slides, both girls were raped.)

Coroner Walter McCarron, still protective of Mrs. Grimes in her anguish over the Madison Street stories about her daughters and her desire that their virtue be preserved, accused Glos of being "publicity mad" and pointed out his lack of expertise in forensic science. "He's mad at me because I want to run for sheriff," Glos shot back. McCarron fired Glos and announced it at a televised news conference of his own.

Bradshaw joined the fracas. It was his angry contention that Glos, whose allegations supported the case against his client, should have presented his evidence or any new information at the inquest. Both he and the ACLU noted the violation of Bedwell's rights, for example, Sheriff Lohman having held him for five days before charging him with a crime. Illinois Senator Robert J. Graham of Chicago charged on the floor of the Senate in Springfield that the police agencies involved in the investigations of both the Grimes and the Schuessler-Peterson cases were withholding information from each other, making resolutions impossible. He demanded that a committee of five senators be named to hold public hearings in Chicago. Senator Arthur J. Bidwill of River Forest maintained that Chicago murders were none of the Senate's business.[22] Unemployed Harry Glos, Lohman's sole ally, went to work for the beleaguered sheriff, sans pay, to help solve the case—ideally and ultimately to bring about a conviction of Bennie Bedwell.

The ugliness pervading the investigation of the double murder was not limited to its professional luminaries. There had been talk that certain neighbors of the Grimes family were concerned that the fund being raised for them was growing too large. Father Schomburg, St. Maurice assistant pastor for sixteen years, spent one of his Sunday sermons in February admonishing parishioners for their "uncharitable attitude" toward the Grimes family, citing their "jealousy and scandalous talk." Praising the "solidarity and familyness in our community of people who have lived together two and three generations," he suggested that those thoughtless parties remedy the situation with a few words of kindness. The priest, counsel and comfort to Mrs. Grimes during the ordeal, exalted her devotion to her seven children and her diligence in caring for them.

Mrs. Grimes was not present at the Mass. "Those who have said unkind things about my family have never said them to my face," she

---

[22] The executive committee of the Illinois Senate would refuse to intervene and vote down the proposed investigation 13 to 8.

responded upon hearing of the priest's admonition. "Most of my neighbors have been good friends," she said, "offering everything they have."

It was Mrs. Grimes who supposedly provided confirmation of the evidence that Barbara and Patricia died December 28th. Newspaper accounts on February 14th reported how, during a meeting with the four pathologists who'd conducted the autopsies, she had a sudden recollection from the afternoon of December 28th. Her son Joey, she revealed, had found ten dollars on the street and had treated Patricia to a banana split. "How could I have forgotten that?" she reportedly exclaimed aloud, prompting the doctors to inform her that they had found a piece of banana in Patricia's intestine. This meeting with the doctors and revelation from Mrs. Grimes occurred on Wednesday, February 13th; however, the story of the banana split had appeared in the newspapers on January 31st.

Things were looking up for Bedwell.

A Most Special Birthday

"I knew Bennie Bedwell had to go free."

> Mrs. Lorretta Grimes, upon hearing of the dismissal of murder charges against Bennie Bedwell.

As February 1957 drew to a close, a flurry of investigative activity filled the papers as though the police were making one last ditch effort to wrap things up, before the whole thing faded out.

On February 22nd, the *Chicago Tribune* reported that a babushka discovered a week earlier near the spot where the sisters' bodies were found resembled those they wore the night they disappeared. The information had been kept from the public, pending laboratory tests.

Joseph Riotta, 2859 South Tripp Avenue, reported to police that he'd seen two girls resembling Barbara and Patricia dragged into a car at Western and Archer avenues on December 28th. Once he made the report, he received a phone call from a man who threatened to kill him if he talked to police again. A police guard was assigned to Riotta's home.

Two clues reported on February 25th were: 1) a paint chip found in the shroud covering one of the girls during transport to the morgue, described as a fleck made up of three layers—red underneath, black in the middle, and gray on top; and 2) matter found underneath the fingernails of the girls, clues for which no follow-up was ever reported.

Then police pulled in several men known to be sexual molesters and questioned them all, getting nowhere.

Two additional McKinley Park residents belatedly reported neighborhood stalking incidents, both involving the Grimes sisters and black and red cars. On February 28th, Francis Suver, 15, reported seeing Barbara and Patricia trailed by a black and red car on December 27th, the night before they disappeared. They were walking south on Leavitt Street, toward 36th Street, where they turned left to head to Damen Avenue, according to Suver.

William Absher, 46, of 3513 South Seeley Avenue, told police he was taking a walk the night of December 28th and saw Barbara and Patricia talking to three boys in a black and red car, which was parked at 35th Street and Damen Avenue. The time of the sighting coincided with their journey to the Brighton Theater to see *Love Me Tender*. Barbara called one of the men "Jack," according to Absher, who said that one of them called after the girls, as they walked away, "You'll be sorry."

Then a surprise from fifteen-year-old Delores Castillo, a classmate who shared a locker with Barbara Grimes at Kelly High School. Delores stepped up to say that Barbara had shown her pictures of a boyfriend she referred to as Eddie. Delores, having seen Bedwell's picture in the newspapers, believed he was the same man. Barbara had indicated that she'd met Eddie, whom she described as a "hillbilly" from Wisconsin who drove a Buick, in September 1955, in a local five and dime store on a school holiday. She had shown Delores one photo of the man, leaning against a car, and another one of him from the waist up. Barbara mentioned him from time to time, according to Delores, stating that they'd had occasional dates and that she was crazy about him. Delores claimed to have not come forward sooner because she was afraid.

Both Mrs. Grimes and Bedwell's attorney countered the story. "Barbara did not date," claimed her mother, "except with a couple of neighborhood boys who would come over." Bradshaw disclosed that Bedwell had been away for much of the time during which he was supposedly dating Barbara, although he was in Chicago briefly that September, then away again until April 1956.

Mr. Bedwell would soon be departing the windy city once again—by a means no one could have guessed.

He'd been working, after his release from jail on February 5th, at a job arranged for him by Bradshaw at Salvation Army Men's Social Center at 509 North Union Avenue. His day began at 6:30 with breakfast, after which he worked in the center's repair shop, painting furniture until 4:00 p.m. In addition to room and board at the agency, the weary ex-prisoner received remuneration of $1 a day. His regimen, which included a 10:00 p.m. curfew, precluded participation in the bawdy nightlife of West Madison Street. Bedwell seemed content with that. "I sure won't go back to those derail[23] cocktails and lady barflies of Skid Row," he vowed. "I've done learned my lesson."

States Attorney Adamowski announced on March 1st that the charges against Bedwell would be dropped at the upcoming hearing on Monday, March 4th. He stated that because of the certainty of the pathologists' findings that the girls died December 28th, witnesses placing them in the company of Bedwell on later dates were well meaning but mistaken. "Their testimony could carry considerable weight," he stated,

---

[23] Perhaps Bedwell, in describing drinks and women, was using Merriam Webster's Collegiate Dictionary's second definition of "derail": "to obstruct the progress of."

"and would, in a sense, 'corroborate' some of the sordid details, if the date of death were uncertain."

Adamowski added in his statement that the sheriff's office had misled him into accepting Bedwell's "seemingly absurd" confession, but despite the criticism, Lohman himself proposed a special jury study "of the conduct by all the law enforcement agencies and investigative bodies involved in the inquiry." While Harry Glos promised to produce a new witness who had firsthand knowledge of Bedwell and the Grimes sisters cavorting together, Adamowski blasted Lohman's request for the study as "an indictment of his [Lohman's] own forces."

Bedwell was feeling pretty good. Photographers found him eating birthday cake and cheerily pondering his plans for the future at the home of his mother on West Monroe Street on Sunday, March 3rd, just one day before he turned twenty-two.

Bedwell's freedom would last about as long as his birthday party. Newspaper stories of the Grimes double murder and Bedwell's arrest circulating around the country had reached Volusia County, Florida. It seems that the sheriff there, Hardie R. Daughtery, had been searching for Bedwell for nearly a year in connection with the rape of a thirteen-year-old girl there. She and a fourteen-year-old friend had met Bedwell and another man at a carnival in DeLand and invited them to her home, where she introduced them to her parents as "Bennie Bedwell" and "Indian John." The girls disappeared after attending a movie with the two men and were reported missing by their fathers the next day. Sheriff's deputies found them three days later in an abandoned trailer on the outskirts of the city, where they'd been left with small amounts of food and a warning from their captors not to leave. They'd been raped and slapped around, and when the Grimes case appeared in the newspapers in DeLand, the thirteen-year-old took clippings to Sheriff Daughtery and identified her attacker as none other than former carnival roustabout Bennie Bedwell. Daughtery decided not to follow through, thinking Bedwell would be charged with murder in Chicago, but upon reading of his release, he contacted Sheriff Lohman and set a warrant in motion.

On Monday, March 4th, a jubilant Bedwell exited the courthouse after hearing the pronouncement that he would not be prosecuted by the State of Illinois for the murders of Barbara and Patricia Grimes. While smiling amiably for photographers, he was rearrested—much to the consternation of his attorney and his mother—on a fugitive warrant from Florida. He was ushered, by Undersheriff Thomas Brennan, into the office of Captain James McCann of the Bedford Park station. Bradshaw, who had pushed his way through the chaos in the building entryway, tried to make his way around a sergeant's desk, shouting, "You can't do this," then, reaching the door to McCann's office, "I demand to see my client; I demand my rights." Despite his attorney's tirade, Bedwell was held inside for twenty-five minutes and came out in handcuffs.

Upon Bedwell's return to court, States Attorney Robert Zadek read a Florida statute providing that rape carried a life imprisonment or death penalty and was not bailable. Justice of the Peace Irving Eiserman set bail nonetheless, at $100,000, the amount laid out in the original warrant, and the once-again prisoner was transported to County Jail.

"My client has no more chance of raising his bail than he has of flying to the moon," stormed the tempestuous Bradshaw, proposing that it was terribly fishy that the Florida warrant would pop up just as Bedwell was about to go free. No rape occurred, he insisted, and the only identification linking Bedwell with the alleged Florida victim was through his photographs.

On March 8th, extradition papers were mailed by Florida Governor Leroy Collins to Illinois Governor William Stratton, who appointed a Springfield attorney to handle the matter. Whether Bedwell would be extradited to the sunshine state would be decided at a March 25th hearing set by Governor Stratton, to be conducted by Paul Hansen of the Illinois Legislative Reference Bureau.

During Bedwell's repeat stay in County Jail, one of his acquaintances from Skid Row, a woman impersonating a man and using the name Ernest Whitley, was herself jailed for assault with a deadly weapon. Whitley, a scavenger truck driver, was heard, through a vent that led from the women's jail to the men's, shouting a conversation about a letter she'd written on behalf of Bedwell to the alleged victim in DeLand, offering to marry her if he had made her pregnant. The letter was written, according to Whitley, in March or April of 1956.

Meanwhile, the witness alluded to earlier by Harry Glos—disguised, having asked that his identity not be revealed—became front-page news on March 10th in the *Chicago American*. The witness, a tree surgeon and Army veteran, was sure he had seen the two sisters on January 5th in a tavern with Bennie Bedwell on Skid Row. The man waited to report what he'd seen until February 20th, when he realized what speaking out had cost the former coroner's assistant. "I figured if Mr. Glos could give up his job for what he thinks is right, I should come forward," he explained.

The man had left an auto show at the International Amphitheater with a friend and driven to Halsted Street, turning left on West Madison Street. Passing the Skid Row section, which was unknown territory for the two men, they decided to stop for a beer at a bar just east of Homan Avenue. They ordered, and a few minutes later, two girls came in and walked straight back to the women's washroom. He described the events as follows:

I made some remark about how young they looked. The girls came back out in a short time. But a few minutes later, one of them—the taller one who wore blue jeans—came back in and sat at the bar. The bar curves and I could see her plainly.

The witness said that the girl drank nothing and soon exited the bar. He and his friend then left, both men drawn by the hillbilly music of the Southern Inn across the street, where they again saw the two girls.

The band was playing, and [they] were dancing together They were in their stocking feet—bobby sox—and were doing a kind of jitterbug step....Again, I noticed how young they looked.

The witness described a "big gorilla of a man" sitting nearby, with sideburns and long hair, as Bennie Bedwell. "I never forget a face," he swore, adding that one of the girls looked him straight in the eyes several times. "That girl was Barbara."

Glos responded.

I sincerely believe this witness is telling the truth. This information has already been passed on to the State's Attorney....I have asked to have this man brought before the grand jury to tell his story. I have further asked the State's Attorney to share the original notes taken during the post mortem—not the abstract of the report, but the full notes—subpoenaed and taken before the grand jury.

I have asked that the color slides of the girls' bodies now in possession of the Chicago police crime laboratory be subpoenaed.

I have asked also that any three neutral forensic pathologists...look over the notes and slides and present their findings to the State's Attorney and the public.

Glos reiterated that he'd been promised complete notes by Dr. Hirsch and had seen nothing but an abstract and that he believed that the slides would answer questions about the postmortem wounds, blood in Patricia's pericardial sac, and indications of violence done to the girls, especially the wounds in Patricia's chest. Glos obviously wasn't backing down in his efforts to see that the truth was exposed concerning violence and sexual molestation of the girls, without which he felt no solution could be attained.

Spurts of investigative activity—fewer and further between—appeared in the news during the month of March like sparks in a dying fire. Gary Lindsay, of Monroe City, Indiana, made calls to the Grimes home and was arrested around the middle of the month. Lindsay had informed Theresa Grimes, by phone, that her sisters' clothes were hidden under a trestle in the Chicago and Eastern Illinois Railroad yards in Dolton, Illinois. He indicated during one call that he feared talking to her at home because her line was tapped. Theresa gave him the number of a nearby restaurant, where he then called her. Police traced the call and took him in for questioning. Lindsay, a nineteen-year-old railroad switchman, was found to be carrying a fountain pen-type container with live tear gas cartridges for which he had no explanation.

April brought no news to speak of, and by summer, it seemed that one could finally get through a day without a thought, or a speculation, about the Grimes sisters. Then there was little fanfare when August brought word from DeLand, Florida, that a jury there had found Bennie Bedwell not guilty of statutory rape.

In October the case made a brief return visit to the newspapers when Mrs. Grimes received a postage due envelope in the mail containing a black rosary and a white bobby sock. Hope surfaced once again when Mrs. Grimes said the sock resembled the bobby socks her daughters wore and brother Jimmy Grimes said that Patricia sometimes borrowed his rosary, which was black. The envelope also contained a piece of paper with notes in blue crayon, which read on one side: "Me see police not get some place remember woman hear girl scream," and on the other: "Me find this in alley Jan 20 boy clean car like crazy 3528 Damen." The address was a vacant lot, and Mrs. Grimes was unable to positively identify the rosary or the sock as belonging to either of her daughters.

The case again faded from the landscape, or so it seemed.

The Aftermath

"I wonder where they'd be today."

> Comment made in the year 2003 by Dora Fisher, viewing a 1956 photograph of friends Barbara and Patricia Grimes.

While the Grimes case eventually disappeared from the news, it has remained in Chicago's collective memory. It takes only a word to revive its sadness and mystery and to conjure up associations to life events: a clerk in the Daley Center who was getting married when it happened; a waitress in a downtown restaurant whose father had just died; a woman on a city bus who recalls the fear she felt at the time, when she was only eight years old.

Marjorie Glen, who grew up on the West Side, was a baby in 1957, but still felt its impact: "I heard about that murder all my life," she says. "It was my mother's reason why we couldn't go out after dark or stay out late. She scared us with it." Linda Modrowski, who was only eight at the time, also remembers the fear. "That murder scared me and my sisters to death," she says today. Modrowski lived on the Southwest Side and remembers her grandmother cutting clippings from the newspapers. Debra Kundert,[24] who was a child living in Willow Springs in the years immediately following the murders, says that her curfews as a teenager were set as a result of the fate of the Grimes sisters.

In the immediate neighborhood where the Grimes sisters lived, an ethnic, close-knit enclave that was slow to change but is now being transformed by gradual gentrification, a more personal recollection still registers shock on the faces of long-time residents: "Oh, yes, I remember those girls," comments one woman somberly. "I saw them over there the night they disappeared." She points to the spot where the Brighton Theater stood[25] and where Barbara and Patricia spent what was possibly their last evening on earth.

Dorothy Weinert DeSaga says that her life, as she knew it, changed once the crime occurred. She was provided with security for eight months after the girls died, and like Rosemarie Rancatore Eggers, she was questioned extensively by police, who followed her everywhere and often intercepted her as she attempted to enter Kelly High School. "Sometimes they would drive me around in their squad cars all day, shooting questions

---

[24] Debra Kundert was a close friend of sixteen-year-old Deborah Rosencrans, who was found unconscious in Schiller Park Woods on September 6, 1977, and not identified until her death twelve days later. Her murder remains unsolved.
[25] The Brighton Theater was torn down in 2002.

at me – 'Did you kill the Grimes sisters?' they would ask. 'Did you have them killed? Are you withholding anything?' Sometimes they gave me money. They even took me to 26th and California[26] once and tried to hypnotize me, but I didn't go under."

DeSaga tells the story of going downtown to the Secretary of State's office to apply for an Illinois State I.D. when she was twenty-one. "The clerk who waited on me looked at my application and repeated my name a few times—'Weinert, Weinert…that name sounds familiar.' Then his face lit up, and he said, 'Were you the girl who knew the Grimes sisters?' I told him I was, and he asked me to accompany him to the back of the office. When we got back there, he showed me photos of Barbara and Patricia lying on the ground on German Church Road. Turns out he'd been a police photographer and had shot the photos himself. It had been six years since the murders, and he still recognized my name. They [the Grimes sisters] became my identity; it became customary to hear, 'Oh, you're the one who knew the Grimes sisters.'" DeSaga says suddenly; "I haven't talked about this in years. After being on TV, on the stand [at the inquest], and hounded by the cops, I just wanted to put it behind me and get on with my life. But," she adds, echoing sentiments of another

---

[26] This is the location of Cook County Jail.

childhood friend of the two girls, Dora Fisher, "it's not something you ever forget. Hearing their names brings it all back, like it was yesterday."

Memories of the crime are not limited to those who knew the girls or lived in their neighborhood, nor are they limited to metropolitan Chicago. In the community where Barbara and Patricia's bodies were found a legacy of rumor and folklore has grown up around this mystery. German Church Road belies the scene of horror that unfolded there nearly fifty years ago. Birds chirping in trees above and the rippling of a brook below suggest tranquility. Before the events of 1957, the name of the stream—Devil's Creek—seemed inappropriate.

Fifty feet or so east of the creek, its entrance blocked with a steel cable, was a narrow gravel drive that once led to a house, occupied by a young family with two small children, until the grisly find on the edge of their property precipitated a hasty flight. Why the family fled the house with only the clothes they were wearing remains as puzzling as "Who killed the Grimes sisters?" and evokes as much speculation.

Furniture and toys littered the yard for years, and a 1955 Buick sat rusting in the driveway. Someone set fire to the house, and the owner had to demolish what was left. The Buick eventually disappeared, carried away piecemeal by vandals.

As recently as 1991 there were remnants of plumbing pipes and hedges in what would have been the side yard, and a kitchen chair lay askew near a severed section of a tricycle. Below an intact wood foundation was a basement still bearing signs of the family life that once existed there. A water heater sat in a far corner; a rusted fuse box remained on one wall; screens, leaning against each other near the remains of a staircase, waited decades to cover windows that no longer existed. A workbench could be seen behind a pile of crumbled flagstone in the center of the floor. A wall held satanic writings and symbols and graffiti that read, ironically, "Pink Floyd. Nobody's home."

Just east of the barren foundation, interrupting land that had gradually been reclaimed by nature, two tires protruded in eerie silence from a pond covered with a motionless layer of pale green algae and overhanging tree branches. Now and then, in winter, when the trees were bare and visibility good, nearby residents observed a tall, gaunt man walking around the grounds. They believed him to be the owner but were afraid to ask. Some think the man was questioned about the killings and felt too conspicuous to stay. Others believe the house was haunted. Some too young to know the story have heard of the long-ago slayings of two girls they assume died inside the "murder house." Police became accustomed to chasing off carloads of teens who drove onto the property to view the place and conduct their mischief, before the barricade was installed across the driveway in the late 1970s.

In the early 1970s, teenagers Terry Wido and Jim Waterstrat enjoyed visiting "so-called spooky places" and made several trips to the house with a group of friends. One of the guys had heard that two girls had been murdered in the house, so to bolster their courage; they took a case of beer. "The lights still worked," he remembers, "and we all posed in the living room with our beers." It was great fun until one night they were approached by dark figures, which began running towards them, prompting them to escape in their car. "We never did go back there," he says, "and years later, I found out that the Grimes sisters were dumped on the road near that house."

In 1982, Jim and Debbie Serpico, a suburban couple, and a group of their friends parked their cars in a nearby church lot and took a Halloween walking tour of the grounds before the house burned, just for fun. Stepping over the barricade, they headed up the driveway toward the house, with only the moon lighting their way. Just as they were debating whether to go inside, they heard a car approach—a dark car with no headlights—that sped past them and disappeared behind the house. Not sure if someone had reported them to police, as locals often did when people visited the grounds, the group opted for a hasty exit. They reached the road only to find the barricade still in place and a policeman parked nearby, who assured them he had seen no car. This is only one of many similar episodes associated with Devil's Creek and the surrounding property over the years. People have reported hearing sounds on the bridge—a car stopping, its doors opening and a noise as though something has dropped before they slam shut and it speeds away.[27]

Today, the remains of the mystery house have been replaced with Bridal Path, an affluent subdivision.

---

[27] Richard T. Crowe, Chicago's original ghost hunter, offers more details in *Chicago's Street Guide to the Supernatural: A Guide to Haunted and Legendary Places in and Near the Windy City,* published in 2000.

Theories

"With the passing years, the mystery has only deepened."

Richard Lindberg,
Author
*Return to the Scene of
the Crime*

Ask five people what happened to the Grimes sisters, and you are likely to receive five different answers. This was a crime that, even minus the jurisdictional ambiguities and power struggles, would have challenged the keenest investigative mind. Every facet of the case presented complexities and multi-tiered mysteries, beginning with the myriad contradictory sightings and questions surrounding the placement of the bodies on German Church Road. Just as you reach a conclusion, a contradiction arises that makes it implausible.

No theory presented explains how the girls were killed or when, which brings up the question of how the bodies lay there on the side of the road for so long without being seen, and where—if they'd been thrown there the day or the night before they were found—they'd been for so long and why there was such extensive damage to their skin by rodents.

Many will express doubt that Bennie Bedwell was responsible for the deaths of the two girls; rather, that he was a patsy grabbed up by authorities to find a quick resolution and make the whole thing go away. How, they wonder aloud, could he have been involved in an abduction between 11:30 p.m. and midnight on December 28th, when he was clearly riding a bus on West Madison Street? Yet, despite the question, there is the nagging possibility that Sheriff Lohman and Harry Glos, both resolute concerning the Tennessee drifter's guilt, may have been onto something.

Lohman and Glos were not the only ones to allude to the connection between the itinerant dishwasher and the victims. In addition to the bevy of seemingly credible witnesses positive they saw them together, an elderly man from the McKinley Park neighborhood, who claimed to have known Chicago police involved in the investigation, spoke of a family cover-up, meant to conceal some less-than-ladylike behavior on the part of the two girls. "They hung around a bar near 36th and Archer," the man claimed, "and older guys would go inside and buy them drinks and deliver them outside. One of those guys," he contended, "was Bennie Bedwell." Could one of his Skid Row buddies have picked up the girls while he made the December 28th bus trip on Madison Street and met up with him later?

It's easy to believe, in reviewing the case, that the accusation leveled against Bedwell in Florida was so similar to what might have befallen the Grimes sisters that his involvement in the Chicago crime is not a stretch. One might also conclude that Bedwell's extradition to Florida was prearranged, that he was, in fact, "given" to authorities there, to put an end to what was an unbearable ordeal for Mrs. Grimes. Nearly everyone involved, including the victims, the police, the coroner, and much of the community, was Catholic. Many resented Lohman and Glos for even thinking Barbara and Patricia capable of taking up with a Skid Row itinerant, considered a lowlife and much older and worldly-wise. Mrs. Grimes may or may not have been privately advised that Bedwell would be tried and presumably convicted in Florida, sparing her more months of torment. Perhaps, with her daughters gone, she was less concerned with Bedwell's fate and primarily concerned with preserving their virtue and good names.

Opinions regarding the characters of the girls are as varied as theories as to how they died. Descriptions such as "a couple of rounders" and "pretty wild" have been ascribed to the two sisters by one investigator in particular and by neighbors who observed them as kids. By one account the two girls "wore provocative clothes in summer and flagged down cars full of boys." By more than one account, they suffered neglect at home, owing to their mother's full time job and problems with alcohol.

Dorothy Weinert DeSaga, supports this portrayal. "When asked if Barbara Grimes was shy as often depicted, DeSaga says emphatically, "Neither one of those girls was shy." Another friend points out the disparity between the amount of freedom allowed the Grimes sisters and their neighborhood chums. To illustrate, DeSaga cites an evening when Barbara and Patricia came to her door to invite her to accompany them on a ride with their cousin in his new car. "Of course, my mother wouldn't let me go," DeSaga says, "it was 10:30 at night, and we were never allowed out that late. The next day, Barbara informed me that the guy they were riding with was not their cousin after all." DeSaga believes that Barbara and Patricia, often left to their own devices by the combination of their mother's long work hours and drinking, were likely to have gotten into a car near 36th Street and Damen Avenue, where they were last seen by Earl Zastro and Ed Lorden—"but not with Bennie Bedwell," she insists. DeSaga remembers Bedwell from the inquest, where she sat next to him. "He smiled and said 'hello' to me, and I remember thinking that he couldn't have been the one. He looked really dull, not someone Barbara and Patricia would have found exciting enough." She concludes, "Their lives were snuffed out at a young age and that was tragic, but a lot of people who knew them thought they were headed for trouble."

Not everyone agrees. Rosemary Chodor Youman, a friend of Theresa Grimes, the girls' older sister, is still angered by negative gossip about Barbara and Patricia, which was not uncommon during the investigation. "That family was held together by love and hard work," she insists. "Barbara and Patricia were nice, ordinary little girls, poor and happy; we all were. Their mother had to work, and she assigned them chores—mopping the floors was one. Our idea of fun was to pour soapy water over them [the floors] and slide around in our bare feet, giggling; silly, little-kid stuff, you know?"

Youman, who last saw her two friends running down Seeley Avenue to visit a deli about 8:30 the night before they disappeared, believes someone in the neighborhood killed them. In response to their alleged escapades on West Madison Street, she draws parameters of a childhood world, extending north and south from 35th Street and Archer Avenue to McKinley Park at 37th Street, and east and west from Seeley to Winchester Avenues. "It was cold that night," she recalls, referring to December 28th. "They might have accepted a ride with someone they knew to get warm; either that or someone forced them into a car."

Robert Lenkart, one of the teens assaulted by local toughs around the time of the girls' disappearance, shares the view that the girls might have known their captors. "They might have gotten into a car with someone they knew," he posits, but without negative insinuations. "After all, we kids were trying to get to know the opposite sex, and that's frequently how we did it." Lenkart lived elsewhere but had a girlfriend in the area and knew Barbara and Patricia slightly—"well enough to know they weren't hanging around in bars," he states with certainty. "They were ordinary teenagers, just like everyone else."

Another debate that has persisted over the years is the possible connection between the Grimes murders and those of the Schuessler brothers and Robert Peterson in 1955, one that Mrs. Grimes strongly accepted. Remarkably, while investigating the disappearance of candy heiress Helen Brach, police ran into evidence related to the murders of the three boys and solved them in 1995, forty years after they occurred. Kenneth Hansen, former stable hand and associate of the late notorious Silas Jayne, was arrested and tried for the murders. Hansen, a known pedophile, was convicted on the basis of the testimony of dubious witnesses. His second trial, held in 2002, ended with the same outcome, however, and he is now serving a 300-year sentence at Pontiac Correctional Center.

While police never questioned Kenneth Hansen about the murders of the Grimes sisters, proponents of the Schuessler-Peterson-Grimes connection quickly point out that his penchant for sex with youngsters may not have been limited to male children, that Hansen might have been the person who forced the two sisters into a car as they approached their house the night they disappeared.

Perhaps they were driven, if not by Hansen, by someone else involved in the Chicago-area equestrian community, to one of the stables located southwest of the city, near Archer Avenue and not far from the site where the bodies were found. A commonly held theory is that they were delivered into a prostitution operation, referred to as a "white slavery ring." Perhaps the girls attempted to escape or were otherwise uncooperative and were killed.

Because of the report of Earl Zastro and Ed Lorden that they observed the two sisters near the intersection of 35th Street and Damen Avenue, it is easy to believe that they were seized near that intersection and would have otherwise been home in just a few minutes. Mrs. Stelle Boske, who lived at 2418 West 35th Street, just about four blocks away, told police she heard "terrifying screams" in the alley behind her house a little after midnight. If Barbara and Patricia were the source of those screams, why were they still in the vicinity? Wouldn't whoever abducted them want to flee the neighborhood as quickly as possible?

It seems that, ultimately, every theory is flawed.

Endings...

Walking around McKinley Park today is like entering a time warp. Archer Avenue is sprinkled with a few fast food restaurants and townhouse developments, but renewal is slow. Modest homes and well-kept two- and three-flat buildings from an earlier time, along with the occasional yard adorned with a statue of Mary Mother of God, continue to characterize the neighborhood. American flags decorate many of the porches. Reactions to gentrification are mixed; one resident, walking with her grandson, points to a church on 36th Street slated for demolition, to be replaced by condominiums. "It's going to be really nice around here," she exclaims pleasantly, while a disgruntled man, who moved away five years ago and is back to visit, laments the scarcity of white faces among neighborhood newcomers and warns me about the criminal element.

The house at 3634 South Damen Avenue, sold and re-sold over the years, appears well cared-for today, its tiny yard colorful with grass and flowers. Its current inhabitants are most likely unaware that their home was once the center of one of Chicago's biggest uproars. Around the corner and two short blocks west is St. Maurice Church, now closed, and the church which I attended with Barbara and Patricia Grimes without ever knowing them. It occurs to me, as I stand in its doorway, that I might have knelt next to their worried mother as she prayed for their safe return. Across the street is the funeral home that serviced them in death, where I became a thoughtless spectator, standing in line to view two closed caskets, locking eyes briefly with a woman whose grief I couldn't, at age sixteen, begin to appreciate. Her sad look of resignation has remained imprinted in my memory over the years, as though caught by the snap of a camera.

Mrs. Grimes died on December 8, 1989, at Westshire Nursing Center, Cicero, Illinois, of congestive heart failure. Following the deaths of her daughters Barbara and Patricia, she continued to live in her house on Damen Avenue until the 1980s, sharing it at times with her son Joey Grimes and his family. During the 1960s, ironically, Mrs. Grimes worked as a matron at Bridewell House of Corrections City Jail. Karl Mattson, a retired Chicago policeman, worked at the jail from February to June 1964, handing out time cards. Mattson remembers greeting Mrs. Grimes each morning, then watching her walk toward the armory, "shoulders hunched, hands together in front, almost as though in prayer, looking as though she carried the weight of her family tragedy."

At the time of her death, she was 83. Rosemary Chodor Youman, childhood friend of the girls, walked into her wake and encountered Theresa Grimes, now Theresa Campanella. "She finally knows who killed them," she said to Theresa.

Mrs. Grimes is buried near her daughters Barbara, Patricia, and Leona at Holy Sepulchre Cemetery in Worth, Illinois.

Joseph C. Grimes, father of Barbara and Patricia, died after suffering a heart attack on June 19, 1965, at age 57, leaving his widow, Grace Wrage Grimes. He, too, is buried in Holy Sepulchre Cemetery.

Edward Lee (Bennie) Bedwell, appeared in Chicago briefly after his acquittal by jury in the statutory rape trial in DeLand, Florida, on August 21, 1957. At some point thereafter, Bedwell migrated to Rantoul, Illinois, where he operated a snake pit ride in a local carnival. On February 4, 1972, he married Virginia Mae Irving, five years his senior, at Miracle Temple Church of God in Christ in Decatur, Illinois. Irving reportedly worked at the same carnival, billed as the "Alligator Lady." The couple moved to St. Louis, Missouri, his wife's home town, where Bedwell worked as a truck driver in the construction industry. His difficult life, as well as his marriage, was short. Afflicted with diabetes mellitus, Bedwell was dead on arrival from heart failure at Barnes Hospital in St. Louis on

November 25, 1972, his new bride's 41st birthday. In death Bedwell occupies grave #2016 in plot J of Jefferson Barracks National Cemetery.

Mr. and Mrs. Curtis Bradberry, mother and stepfather of Bennie Bedwell, occupied several addresses on the near West Side of Chicago, beginning in 1951. On September 15, 1962, Mrs. Bradberry, seriously overweight and diabetic, died at age 49 of primary bronchial pneumonia at Cook County Hospital. She was buried on September 19th at Pleasant Ridge Cemetery in Big Sandy, Tennessee, just southeast of Paris. At the time of her death she had three grandchildren and five step grandchildren.

Mrs. Bradberry left behind her husband Curtis and their eleven-year-old daughter Shirley, who continued to move from one West Side address to another. In 1969 Mr. Bradberry's name disappeared from the Chicago phone directory. The building at 1430 West Monroe Street, in which the family lived when Mrs. Bradberry's son became headline news, is now the site of a parking lot for Chicago's Office of Emergency Management and Communications at 1411 West Madison Street. Like many of the street's buildings, the three-story white limestone had been made into a rooming house and, in great disrepair, was torn down during the 1980s.

Three additional former addresses of the Bradberry family are parking lots, and two have been obliterated by the United Center, built in 1992. The rest, both before and after Mrs. Bradberry died, hold spanking new brick dwellings, home to models of Chicago's prosperous young professionals whose affluence is restoring the inner city to its early twentieth century splendor.

Curtis Bradberry died in Camden, Tennessee, on February 9, 1985. He was 88 years old.

John E. Bedwell, Bennie's older brother, died in Garden City, Kansas, May 2, 1983, after a long illness. Attending his funeral was friend Stella Eichenhauer, who paid all funeral and burial expenses. According to Mr. Bedwell's obituary and Phillips-White Funeral Home records in Garden City, there were no known relatives.

David E. Bradshaw, Attorney for Bennie Bedwell, was a colorful, industrious criminal and insurance lawyer, who, during his career, managed to win freedom for twenty-five out of twenty-six of his clients accused of murder. In 1970, President Nixon appointed Bradshaw as one of the original incorporators of the National Railroad Passenger Corporation, which established Amtrak. He remained on Amtrak's board for three years.

Four-times wed, Bradshaw's most famed marriage was to wealthy W. Clement Stone's daughter, Donna, which lasted five years and ended in a contentious divorce. Bradshaw joined his father-in-law in many enterprises, including production of the television show, *The New Zoo Review.*

Bradshaw resided at several Chicago North Side addresses over the years, including the posh downtown Lake Point Towers. After living for a decade in Arizona, Bradshaw spent the last year of his life battling cancer and counseling others with the disease. He died at his daughter's home in Northbrook, Illinois, on February 18, 1990, at the age of 62.

Sheriff Joseph Dean Lohman, despite his failure to solve the Grimes case, was an accomplished intellect ahead of his time in his knowledge and understanding of social problems. During the 1930s he and his wife Fern lived among Chicago's poor blacks and Italians, in order to gain firsthand information about urban problems, police work, and politics. He served on the faculty of University of Chicago from 1939 to 1959, where he was a dedicated and inspiring teacher. In addition to holding numerous positions in Illinois law enforcement, he organized and directed the first major study of race relations in the federal government, undertaken during the 1940s by the National Commission on Segregation. He served under

Presidents Truman and Eisenhower as chairman of the National Planning Commission for Washington, DC, and helped establish the Southern Police Institute in Louisville, Kentucky. In 1958, following his term as Cook County Sheriff, he was elected Treasurer of the State of Illinois.

Unfortunately, Lohman's political aspirations clouded his judgment, and despite a friendly relationship with the press, he developed a less than esteemed public image after the Grimes case fiasco. As predicted during his controversial tenure as sheriff, Lohman ran for governor of Illinois as an Independent in 1960. In gearing up for the political battle, Lohman was asked by Jake Arvey, party big shot, where he attended church. Upon learning that Lohman was not a practicing "anything" but was Jewish, Arvey instructed him to establish an affiliation with a temple. It was therefore said that "Arvey made a Jew out of Lohman." His staged religious devotion was not enough to bring in sufficient votes, however, and the aspiring governor lost the election.

Lohman was Dean of the School of Criminology at Berkeley at the time of his death, at age 58, in 1969. His wife passed away July 5, 1991.

Harry L. Glos was assistant coroner at the time of the Schuessler-Peterson murders, the yet-unsolved murder of Judith Mae Andersen,[28] and the intervening Grimes case. The son of Harry Glos, Sr., editor of *Village Events*, a suburban newspaper, Glos had quite an extensive history in law enforcement. In 1941, as a state trooper, he worked with a motorcycle team protecting celebrities who received death threats during war bond drives. The team, known as the Four Horsemen, also performed stunts on their Harley 74s.

Before joining the coroner's office in 1953, Glos had also been a Forest Park patrolman and sergeant for the Oak Park Police Department. When McCarron terminated his position as coroner's assistant during the Grimes investigation, Glos continued to work on the case gratis and started his own private detective agency. He later served as chief of police for the Village of Northlake.

Six-foot-one, over two hundred pounds, and by all accounts aggressive and forceful in matters of police work, Glos had an artistic and tender side; he was a commercial lettering artist who drew cartoons for the children's wards of area hospitals for nearly half a century.

---

[28] No one was ever tried for the murder of fifteen-year-old Judith Mae Andersen.

Glos retired for health reasons in 1986. After suffering a series of strokes, he died in May of 1994, still convinced that Bennie Bedwell was the culprit in the Grimes murder case.

Walter E. McCarron, elected coroner in 1952, was the first Republican to hold that office since 1928. While serving two four-year terms, he was embroiled in the turf wars of the Schuessler-Peterson and Grimes mysteries, the dismemberment murder of Judith Mae Andersen in August 1957, as well as the investigations of the deaths of merchandising heir Montgomery Ward Thorne and Charles H. Weber, a former alderman in the 45th Ward. Prior to entering politics, McCarron was in the trucking business with his father and was executive director of the Illinois Motor Truck Operators Association. He lived in Oak Park until he retired to Ft. Lauderdale, Florida. He was visiting relatives in Chicago at the time of his death, at age 85, at Little Company of Mary Hospital in Evergreen Park. He'd been married to his grade-school sweetheart for sixty years.

Robert J. Cooney, Sr., prosecutor in the case against Bennie Bedwell, died of cancer at Northwestern Memorial Hospital on February 11, 1995. Cooney had served in the U.S. Army and was awarded the Bronze Star for valor in combat, before beginning his legal career in the 1950s with the states attorney's office. In 1958, he went into private practice, founding the personal injury law firm of Cooney and Stenn and later was joined in his practice by his two sons, John and Robert, Jr. Cooney was 70 years old when he died.

William Cole Willingham, Bennie Bedwell's drinking buddy and the man known as "Frank," who was implicated in the murders of Barbara and Patricia Grimes by Bedwell's confession, died in Los Angeles, California. At the time of his sudden death of a heart attack on October 14, 2002, he was 71 and had no known living relatives.

Richard William Whittemire, young man reportedly seen with Bennie Bedwell and the Grimes sisters at the D & L Restaurant on December 30, 1956, died March 25, 1999, in Knoxville, Tennessee, after a long illness. The United States Airforce veteran was 70 years old. There was no wake, and no relatives were in attendance at his graveside service on March 31, 1999, at Greenwood Cemetery.

John and Minnie Duros, the couple who owned the Skid Row D & L Restaurant, were 69 and 68 respectively in 1957, when they swore that Bennie Bedwell had visited their diner with Barbara and Patricia Grimes. Mr. Duros died in December 1971 at age 83, and his wife died in September 1974 at age 82. Their home at 3256 West Warren Boulevard has been razed and replaced by a new brick condominium building.

Joseph Smok, CTA bus driver who identified Barbara and Patricia Grimes as passengers the night they disappeared, died December 1982 in Burbank, Illinois.

Joseph Gagliano, the Memphis police inspector who spoke to *Chicago Daily News* reporters about the practice of teenage girls visiting Tennessee to catch a glimpse of Elvis Presley died of a sudden heart attack on January 14, 1979. At the time of his death he was chief of police in Germantown, Tennessee, a suburb of Memphis.

Roger L. Menard, who sat behind and observed Barbara and Patricia Grimes in the Brighton Theater as they watched *Love Me Tender* on December 28, 1956, and walked behind them as they made their way down Archer Avenue, died on January 23, 1996, en route Holy Cross Hospital. Menard, in retail sales and never married, was 58 years old.

Walter Henry Kranz, prophetic dreamer and first suspect in the Grimes case, was a resident of the Englewood neighborhood of Chicago. Forty-five at the time of the murders[29], he no doubt moved away from the Southwest Side area, which saw great racial transformation during the sixties. Neither he nor any of his relatives could be located.

---

[29] Born in 1911, Kranz was younger in 1957 than reported in newspapers.

Pearl Neville, probably in her fifties at the time of the Grimes sisters' murders, was never heard of after she made her 1957 Greyhound bus excursion and unexpected layover in Chicago. It is unlikely that she saw the two girls in Nashville as she claimed, but for a brief moment, she provided hope for their anxious mother. Despite searches on the Internet and conversations with various Nevilles in the state of Minnesota, no relatives or record of her whereabouts could be found.

Leonard and Marie Prescott continued to live a few miles down the road from the site where Mr. Prescott discovered the bodies of the Grimes sisters, in the same home they occupied when the crime occurred, until they both died just ninety days apart. Marie died at age 81 on March 4, 2005 (Bennie Bedwell's birthday), after a fall from which she never recovered. For many years she had cared for her husband, Leonard, who was diabetic and virtually blind. Leonard died of pneumonia after a bout of flu on May 22nd. He was 89.

The couple, married since 1942, were no strangers to hard work and struggle—or to heartbreak. Ironically, since the tragic events of 1957, in which they were haplessly ensnared, they lost two children of their own.

It was Mrs. Prescott's strong contention that Bennie Bedwell killed Barbara and Patricia Grimes. "I know that guy was guilty," she stated in

2002, a theory she apparently developed upon her observation of him at the inquests. She claimed also that she and her husband had reported horse tracks around the spot where they found the bodies and that she felt strong resentment that those reports seemed to not be taken seriously. She also resented that police aggressively intruded on the couple's lives after they reported their grim finding on January 22, 1957. "I can't even mention this to Leonard," she said, "he's getting on in years, and it upsets him so." She added that she couldn't drive across Devil's Creek without thinking of a day long ago when she made a simple request of her husband that changed their lives so dramatically.

Had the girls not died, their paths would most likely not have crossed with the Prescotts. In fact, most of us would never have become aware of Barbara and Patricia Grimes, two ordinary kids who figured on ordinary lives and whose names survive only as subject matter for media anniversaries.

Four years after the murders, Channel 9 Chicago News presented an interview with two detectives still working on the case and a rerun of the public plea of Mrs. Grimes to her children's captor to return them unharmed—"If whoever took my girls will just let them go, I'll forgive them from the bottom of my heart."

To realize that someone, somewhere, might have watched, guilty and unmoved, is to know that our label of the fifties as a time of innocence is a misnomer.

CHRONOLOGY

December 28, 1956

> ➤ *Love Me Tender*, Elvis Presley's first movie, begins its run at the Brighton Theater, 4223 South Archer Avenue.

> ➤ Barbara and Patricia Grimes eat dinner at home and leave for the Brighton Theater at 7:15 p.m.

> ➤ Mrs. Lorretta Grimes, mother of Barbara and Patricia, becomes alarmed when the two girls fail to arrive home by 11:30 p.m. She sends a son and another daughter to the bus stop to wait for them; calls police when they fail to appear on three buses.

December 29, 1956

> ➤ A bus driver on Archer Avenue reports seeing two girls leave his bus at Archer and Western Avenues at 11:10 p.m. December 28th. He believes the girls were the Grimes sisters.

➤ A security guard believes two girls he encountered at Lawrence and Central Park Avenues early in the morning are the Grimes sisters.

January 2, 1957

➤ Police, following a lead provided by an unnamed informant, search for two sailors seen with two girls playing Elvis Presley songs in the record department in a 63rd Street Kresge.

January 4, 1957

➤ Joseph Grimes, father of the missing sisters, enlists the help of his truck drivers' union to aid in the search.

➤ Police administer a lie detector test to eighteen-year-old Leona Marlow of the Southwest Side, who reported seeing the Grimes sisters on two different days. The test is inconclusive.

➤ A junk dealer reports seeing two teen girls in Gilman, Illinois, in a maroon colored car with Tennessee license plates and a Chicago vehicle sticker.

➤ A Chicago towing service operator reports seeing two soldiers and two girls resembling the Grimes sisters at a filling station at 2734 North Cicero Avenue at 7:00 a.m.

January 10, 1957

- ➤ Switchboard operator Henrietta Marshall receives a call at the C.Y.O. on South Wabash Avenue from a man who claims to have a teenage girl tied up in his car in the downtown underground parking garage. Police search and find no one.

- ➤ Mrs. Lorretta Grimes makes a television plea to whoever is holding her daughters to let them call her.

- ➤ Mrs. Grimes uses the portable radios Barbara and Patricia received for Christmas and left behind as evidence that they haven't left home voluntarily.

January 11, 1957

- ➤ Search enters its third week.

January 14, 1957

- ➤ Special police force begins house-to-house canvass.

- ➤ Two late-night phone calls are received at the home of Mr. and Mrs. Wallace Tollstan, whose daughter Sandra is a classmate of Patricia Grimes. Mrs. Tollstan believes the voice is that of Patricia.

- ➤ George Pople, manager of Unity Hotel at 750 West 61st Street, says he refused a room to two girls on January 2nd, because they were too young. He believes the girls were Barbara and Patricia Grimes.

January 15, 1957

- Chicago police and Sante Fe Railroad detectives search thousands of railway freight cars for the missing girls. Police also search garages, sheds, and other side houses in the Southwest Side area.

- Police receive a call from a man claiming to have seen the bodies of the two missing girls in Sante Fe Park "in a dream." Police trace the call to Walter Kranz, steamfitter for the railroad, and bring him in for questioning. Kranz first denies, then admits, making the call and states that psychic powers run in his family.

January 16, 1957

- As the search continues and widens for the missing Grimes sisters, 54-year-old Pearl Neville from St. Paul, Minnesota, reports having seen them in a Nashville, Tennessee, washroom and accompanying them to a state employment agency there to apply for work.

January 18, 1957

- Rock 'n' roll singer Elvis Presley issues a statement to the Grimes sisters, believed to be traveling to Nashville to see him, to "go home and ease your mother's worries."

➢ Daily News report states that the city has spent nearly $45,000 in search of the Grimes sisters.

January 19, 1957

➢ Police conduct a futile search of a Pennsylvania train at Englewood station, following a report that the Grimes sisters were passengers.

January 22, 1957

➢ Frozen, nude bodies of two girls, believed to be the missing Grimes sisters, found by suburban resident on German Church Road near County Line Road.

➢ Mrs. Grimes hears of the finding of the bodies and heads for St. Maurice Church in tears. Convinced the girls are her daughters, she cries, "They [the police] wouldn't believe me."

January 23, 1957

➢ Headlines confirm that the bodies discovered on German Church Road are those of Barbara and Patricia Grimes. The girls had been missing twenty-six days.

➢ Police again question Walter Kranz, noting proximity of both Kranz' address and 63rd Street shopping center where the sisters were sighted and of Sante Fe Park and the death site. Police also implicate Kranz in a ransom note received by Mrs. Grimes. He is held for lie detector tests and a psychiatric exam.

January 24, 1957

➢ Sheriff Lohman reports a mystery suspect, arrested at Star–Garter Theater on West Madison Street. The man in question has been identified by three witnesses as the escort of the Grimes sisters in a greasy spoon on West Madison Street.

➢ A fund to help the Grimes family is set up by the Back of the Yards Council.

January 25, 1957

➢ Newspapers identify the new suspect as "West Side Romeo," Tennessee drifter Edward Lee Bedwell, known as "Bennie."

➢ Bennie Bedwell denies being with the Grimes sisters.

➢ Two girls from Grand Rapids, Michigan, come forward and admit that they rather than the Grimes sisters were with Bennie Bedwell and an unidentified second man on Skid Row.

➢ Lorretta Grimes receives donations sufficient to pay off the mortgage on her home at 3634 South Damen Avenue.

➢ A wake for Barbara and Patricia Grimes with closed caskets begins at Wollschlager Funeral Home at 3604 South Hoyne Avenue.

January 26, 1957

- Bennie Bedwell admits carousing with the Grimes sisters with two other men—Frank and Louis—whom he claims knocked the girls out during a scuffle and threw them onto German Church Road.

- Bennie Bedwell then claims he took part in the killing.

- Pawnshop owner reports that two girls wearing clothes resembling that worn by the Grimes sisters tried to hock a watch in his store. He failed to report the incident for three weeks because he was out of town.

- Hundreds attend the wake for Barbara and Patricia Grimes at Wollschlager Funeral Home.

January 27, 1957

- Bennie Bedwell signs a fourteen-page confession.

- A forty-car cavalcade follows Sheriff Lohman and Bennie Bedwell to the death site to reenact the murders of the Grimes sisters.

- Police locate drinking buddy William C. Willingham, Jr., who admits carousing with Bennie Bedwell but denies any part in the killings.

- Mrs. Curtis Bradberry, mother of Bennie Bedwell, enlists the services of Attorney David E. Bradshaw to represent her son.

January 28, 1957

- ➢ Witness fails to identify William Willingham as the man seen with Bennie Bedwell and the Grimes sisters.

- ➢ Barbara and Patricia are laid to rest in Holy Sepulchre Cemetery, Worth, Illinois.

- ➢ Parents of the pallbearers are terrified when someone calls them to say they will never see their daughters alive again.

January 29, 1957

- ➢ Dr. Walter J. R. Camp announces at the inquest that the Grimes sisters died within five hours after leaving home December 28th, invalidating the confession of Bennie Bedwell.

- ➢ Roger L. Menard, 19, reports following Barbara and Patricia Grimes down Archer Avenue after leaving the Brighton Theater December 28th and seeing boys in cars stopping to talk to them.

January 30, 1957

- ➢ Bedwell retracts his confession, claiming police coercion and abuse.

- ➢ Bedwell is denied bail by Justice of the Peace Irving J. Eiserman, because the jury has not yet returned its verdict.

- Earl Zastro and Edward Lorden report seeing the Grimes sisters two blocks from home at around 11:30 p.m. on December 28th.

January 31, 1957

- Bedwell details abuse and bribes by sheriff's police.

- Back of the Yards Neighborhood Council offers $1,000 reward to assist in the investigation.

February 1, 1957

- Ralph Saylor, 26, interviewed at his home at 3338 West Adams Street, tells police he rode the Madison Street bus with Bennie Bedwell after work the night of December 28th, providing Bedwell an alibi for the night Barbara and Patricia Grimes disappeared.

February 2, 1957

- Chief Justice Wilbert F. Crowley sets $20,000 bond for Bennie Bedwell and continues case until February 19th.

- Sheriff Lohman is questioned about his handling of the Grimes murder investigation.

February 3, 1957

- Truck driver Daniel W. Eshelman reports seeing two teenage girls enter an automobile with three men on Archer and Western Avenues on December 28th.

- Police, concentrating their efforts on the McKinley Park neighborhood, pick up three local gang members for questioning.

- Father George Schomburg of St. Maurice Church reprimands the parish members for speaking ill of the Grimes family.

- Aaron Brown, Sr., Mayor of Paris, Tennessee, arrives in Chicago to aid Bennie Bedwell in his legal battle and to help him set up a new life when he's freed.

February 4, 1957

- Police investigate the words "HELP" scrawled on the wall of an abandoned shack on County Line Road.

- Morris Brown, bondsman, heads to Chicago from Champaign, Illinois, to put up the bond for Bennie Bedwell.

- Four local boys are held for lie detector tests after denying any connection to the Grimes murders.

- A newspaper story reveals that Sheriff Lohman has held witness Richard W. Whittemire, drinking buddy of Bennie Bedwell, in the Park Row Hotel, 4144 Roosevelt Road, for questioning. Whittemire first admitted riding the bus with Bennie Bedwell after work on December 28th and meeting an Indian girl in a tavern on Skid Row, but later claimed he couldn't remember the date.

February 5, 1957

- ➢ Bedwell is freed on $20,000 bond raised by Morris Brown, bondsman from Champaign, Illinois.

- ➢ Bennie Bedwell leaves court with his attorney David Bradshaw in a pink Cadillac, heading for a press conference at Belden-Stratford Hotel.

- ➢ Dr. Jerry Kearns inadvertently mentions an oval-shaped wound on the scalp of Patricia Grimes.

- ➢ For the first time since January 23, 1957, news related to the Grimes case fails to appear on the front page of the *Chicago Sun-Times*.

February 6, 1957

- ➢ Sheriff Lohman travels to Alabama to follow up on a secret lead based on two letters received from residents of that area.

- ➢ At a press conference arranged by his attorney at Belden Stratford Hotel, Bennie Bedwell reveals plans to give up his sordid life on Skid Row and take a job at Salvation Army.

- ➢ Mrs. Lorretta Grimes received an anonymous phone call from a woman who said that on February 5th she'd seen two men with sideburns in a black Mercury at Taylor and Halsted Streets with two girls who looked like her daughters.

February 7, 1957

➢ Stanley Zdziarski, car salesman, tells police he saw a girl wearing clothing resembling that worn by Barbara Grimes talking outside his residence to a man in a black Mercury around midnight on December 28th.

February 8, 1957

➢ Due to an elimination of other causes, pathologists announce that the Grimes sisters died of exposure.

➢ Two men who'd been jailed for vagrancy in Georgia visit the Grimes home and report meeting a prisoner who expressed fear that his Mercury might have been used to abduct the Grimes sisters.

February 9, 1957

➢ Pathologists raise the possibility that the Grimes sisters were knocked unconscious and left on the ground to freeze.

February 10, 1957

➢ Police find several items near the site where the Grimes sisters were found and take them to their mother for identification. None is recognized as belonging to the girls.

February 11, 1957

➢ Another inquest session is held, in which Mrs. Grimes presents a list of questions to the coroner's jury.

➢ The jury's verdict states that the Grimes sisters died "from and as a result of secondary shock and exposure to low temperatures…"

February 12, 1957

➢ Police hunt for three teens in a dark Mercury who reportedly tried to crash a party in the Grimes neighborhood December 28th.

February 13, 1957

➢ William Absher of the McKinley Park neighborhood tells police he saw the Grimes sisters meet three young men at 35th Street and Damen Avenue the night they disappeared – prior to the time they attended the movie – and that one of the men shouted, as the girls walked away, "You'll be sorry".

February 14, 1957

➢ Harry Glos, chief investigator of Coroner Walter McCarron, announces a cover-up in the Grimes murders investigation and challenges medical findings that the Grimes sisters died December 28th.

February 15, 1957

➢ Coroner Walter McCarron fires Harry Glos for his public remarks challenging the pathologists' findings.

February 16, 1957

➢ Pathologist Dr. Kearns disputes Harry Glos' assertion that Barbara Grimes was molested.

➢ Pathologists report that banana fibers were found in Patricia Grimes' intestine (Patricia reportedly ate a banana split on the afternoon of December 28th).

➢ Leonard Prescott finds a muddy wallet, initially thought to belong to one of the Grimes sisters, near the death site.

February 17, 1957

➢ Chicago Police Commander Timothy J. O'Connor orders a review of the Grimes case.

February 18, 1957

- Sheriff Joseph Lohman hires ousted Harry Glos to work for him on the Grimes case without pay.

- Four youths in the Grimes neighborhood, who admit getting drunk and attacking a thirteen-year-old girl, are questioned regarding the Grimes murders.

- Police re-interview Walter Kranz, the man who claimed to have dreamed the Grimes sisters lay dead in Sante Fe Park a week before they were found.

February 20, 1957

- Senator Robert Graham asks that a special committee of senators be named to probe the handling of the Grimes murders investigation.

February 21, 1957

- Joseph Riotta reports seeing two girls resembling the Grimes sisters dragged into an automobile at Archer and Western Avenues on December 28th. A police guard is placed at his home after he receives threatening phone calls from a man who warns him to keep silent about the sighting.

February 22, 1957

> ➤ The *Chicago Tribune* reports that a babushka discovered near the death site is being tested to determine if it belonged to one of the Grimes sisters.

February 25, 1957

> ➤ Newspapers report a small flake of paint found in the shroud wrapped around one of the girls for transport to the morgue.

> ➤ Police question Joseph Petrokowitz, 33, in connection with crimes against women and children, including the Grimes case. Petrokowitz is reportedly a friend of Bennie Bedwell.

February 26, 1957

> ➤ Kenneth Renfrow, 24, identified as having tried to pull a woman from her car, is questioned regarding the Grimes murders.

February 27, 1957

> ➤ Delores Castille, friend of Barbara Grimes, reports to police that Barbara carried a photo of Bennie Bedwell in her wallet and identified him as her boyfriend. Mrs. Grimes declares that Barbara did not date.

February 28, 1957

➤ Francis Suver, 15, reports a mystery car following the Grimes sisters on December 28th on Archer Avenue.

March 1, 1957

➤ State's Attorney Benjamin Adamowski announces that murder charges against Bennie Bedwell will be dropped.

March 2, 1957

➤ Sheriff Lohman requests that a special grand jury and prosecutor be set up to study the principles involved in the Grimes investigation.

March 3, 1957

➤ Bennie Bedwell enjoys cake at a birthday party at the home of his mother.

March 4, 1957

➤ This is Bedwell's stated 22nd birthday (his birth certificate lists his actual birth date as March 4, 1936, which would have made him twenty-one). He is freed from charges in the Grimes case and is rearrested on a fugitive warrant for rape of a teenage girl in DeLand, Florida.

March 7, 1957

➤ Chief Justice Wilbert Crowley dismisses a habeas corpus petition by Bedwell's attorney David Bradshaw, and Bedwell is taken back to jail.

March 8, 1957

➤ Extradition papers for the DeLand rape charge are mailed to Florida's Governor Leroy Collins.

➤ Ernest Whitley, 27-year-old woman who dresses as a man, reveals by shouting through a cell air vent in County Jail that she wrote a letter on Bedwell's behalf, in which he offered to marry the alleged Florida rape victim if he had made her pregnant.

August 12, 1957

➤ The home of Mrs. Lorretta Grimes is ransacked by burglars who break through a kitchen window and take $120.00 from a bureau drawer.

August 21, 1957

➤ Bennie Bedwell is found not guilty by a jury in his trial for statutory rape of a thirteen-year-old girl in DeLand, Florida.

August 23, 1957

➢ Bedwell shows up in Chicago, claiming he's going to rest for a month.

➢ Mrs. Irene Haubrek, 65, is sent to Manteno State Hospital following her phone calls to the home of Mrs. Grimes.

October 22, 1957

➢ Mrs. Grimes receives an envelope in the mail, postage due, containing a black rosary, a white bobby sock, and a note written in blue crayon on both sides of a piece of paper. She is unable to positively identify the items as belonging to either of her daughters.

June 19, 1965

➢ Joseph C. Grimes, father of Barbara and Patricia Grimes, dies of a heart attack at the age of 57. He is buried in Holy Sepulchre Cemetery in Worth, Illinois.

February 4, 1972

➢ Bennie Bedwell, 35, marries Virginia Mae Irving, 40, at the Miracle Temple Church of God in Christ, in Decatur, Illinois. It is Bedwell's first marriage, his bride's second.

November 25, 1972

➤ Bennie Bedwell is dead on arrival at Barnes Hospital in St. Louis, Missouri, from heart failure, at age 36, on the 41st birthday of his bride Virginia Mae Irving Bedwell. He is buried four days later in Jefferson Barracks National Cemetery.

May 2, 1983

➤ Johnny E. Bedwell, 53, brother of Bennie Bedwell, dies in Garden City, Kansas. His funeral is attended by one friend, Stella Eichenauer, and no relatives.

December 8, 1989

➤ Mrs. Lorretta Grimes dies, at age 83, of congestive heart failure at Westshire Nursing Center in Cicero, Illinois. She is buried near her daughters, Barbara, Patricia, and Leona in Holy Sepulchre Cemetery in Worth, Illinois.

REFERENCES

Back of the Yards Neighborhood Council.
http://www.bync.org/history background/index.cfm.

Chicago's four daily newspapers: *Chicago Daily Tribune; Chicago Sun-Times; Chicago American; Chicago Daily News.*

Crowe, Richard T., with Carol Mercado. *Chicago's Street Guide to the Supernatural: A Guide to Haunted and Legendary Places in and Near the Windy City.* Chicago: Carolando Press, Inc., October 2000.

GPNWS Interviews.
http://streetlevel.iit.edu/youthprojects/chs/nws/edg.html, 5/11/2004.

Grossman, J.R., Keating, A.D., & Reiff, J.L. (Eds.) *The Encyclopedia of Chicago.* Chicago: University of Chicago Press, 2004.

History of the Illinois State Comptroller's Office,
www.ioc.state.il.us/Office/history.cfm.

Lindberg, Richard C. (1999) *Return to the Scene of the Crime*, Nashville, TN, Cumberland Publishing House.

Lindberg, Richard C. (2001) *Return* Again *to the Scene of the Crime*, Nashville, TN, Cumberland Publishing House.

Lindberg, Richard C. (1991) *To Serve and Collect: Chicago Politics and Police corruption from the Lager Beer Riot to the Summerdale Scandal.* New York: Praeger Publishers.

North, Gary. Guys Didn't Scream for Elvis.
http://www.lewrockwell.com/north/north121.html, 2002.

William Morris Bioff, *Wikipedia, The Free Encyclopedia*
http://en.wikipedia.org/wiki/William_Morris_Bioff, 7/01/2005.

Young, Thomas J. (1989) Indigent Alcoholics on Skid Row. In Lawson, G. & Lawson, A. (Eds) *Alcoholism and Substance Abuse in Special Populations*, Rockville, MD: Aspen Publishers.

About The Author

Tamara Shaffer, originally from Western Pennsylvania, has lived in the Chicago area for nearly fifty years. After raising three children, she began writing as a hobby in 1989 while raising a grandson. Her articles, short stories, and book reviews have appeared in magazines, newspapers, and journals, including *Woman's World, Chicago Tribune, Chicago Sun-Times, Chicago Reader, Today's Chicago Woman, Chicago Life, Phoebe, and the Pedestal Magazine*. She is author of *Tracking Down Mr. Right*, a book of short romance stories. She is retired and has seven grandchildren and one great grandchild.

COMING SOON FROM THE GHOST RESEARCH SOCIETY PRESS

FIELD GUIDE HAUNTED CHURCHES, SYNAGOGUES and CATHEDRALS
"Ghostly activity on Sacred Grounds from across the U.S."
By Dale Kaczmarek

FIELD GUIDE TO HAUNTED BED & BREAKFASTS
Ghostly Tales & Haunted Sites for those staying the night.
By Jim Graczyk

And don't Miss Any Books in the Series by
Visiting the Ghost Research Society Press at:
http://www.ghostresearch.org/press.html